T34

This book is due for return on or before the last date shown below.

Four-minute Smiler

THE DEREK IBBOTSON STORY

To
my mother
MRS. MABEL IBBOTSON

The champ and the ex-champ. Herb Elliott chats with Ibbotson a few days after the Australian had wrested the world mile title from him in 1958

Four-minute Smiler

THE DEREK IBBOTSON STORY

As told by

TERRY O'CONNOR

STANLEY PAUL
London

STANLEY PAUL & CO. LTD
178–202 Great Portland Street, London, W.1

AN IMPRINT OF THE  HUTCHINSON GROUP

London Melbourne Sydney
Auckland Bombay Toronto
Johannesburg New York

First published 1960

*This book has been set in Times New Roman type
face. It has been printed in Great Britain by the
Anchor Press, Ltd., in Tiptree, Essex, on Antique
Wove paper and bound by Taylor Garnett Evans
& Co., Ltd., in Watford, Herts*

Contents

Illustrations

Foreword

BY HERB ELLIOTT

During my visit to England for the Empire Games I was fortunate enough to stay with Derek Ibbotson and his wife, and also Terry O'Connor and his wife. I feel happy to say we all formed close friendships. I saw Derek as an athlete, family man, golfer and a salesman. In the topsy-turvy stay I had with Terry I developed a great respect for one of the best sports writers in the world.

Nevertheless, I was surprised to receive an invitation to write this foreword. As a writer, my powers are usually confined to letters, and I find even these a strain at times. But I shall endeavour to make it known to you in a limited way, as is only possible here, the work, sacrifices and disappointments Derek had to go through to gain a world record for his country and himself. Then I will draw a sketch of Derek as a man and conclude with an opinion (which I always find extremely dangerous) on the future of 'The Mile'. You must realize, of course, that you are getting this forecast from an athlete, which, I am often told by non-athletes, means that you get a twisted point of view.

Let me begin with the Landy-Bannister saga. This was the introduction to the modern era of mile running. I do not believe I am being outspoken in saying that until this time the Blue Riband event on every athletic programme was the 100 yards. Then these two men, who both had a large dash of natural ability for middle-distance running, began to realize that the four-minute mile was only a psychological barrier. How much harder it is to do something which we believe is impossible! Bannister and Landy trained themselves to a state of fitness which possibly only the longer-distance runners had previously attained. As these men neared the 'impossible' the newspapers took up the cry, and the four-minute mile became talked about around the bar, in the household and, of course, on the athletics track. Public interest was aroused all over the world, in particular Britain and Australia. It was a race to see who would attain the goal first. I know that interest was at a terrific pitch in Australia. Never had crowds at athletics meetings been bigger. Then, in a wonderful run, Bannister reached the magic target. Soon afterwards Landy ran an even faster time. Landy was the hero of Australia.

You might wonder what I am driving at. It's this. When Ibbotson overcame a field of the world's best milers to run 3 min. 57·2 sec. he was talked about all over Australia, and probably the world. I knew Derek as the 'cheeky Yorkshireman' of the newspapers. I respected him as a man who had done something better than anyone had achieved before him. I must admit I thought of Derek as a superman. This form of idolatry, which is a perfectly natural reaction, is something I have now learned to hate. I must apologize for using myself to illustrate the point. I have met many people since I have achieved success in athletics who clasped me with a fervent handshake and made me feel like a prize monkey. Well, perhaps I am. I don't mind that, but as many of these people discovered I was just an ordinary person who runs a bit, the pedestal was smashed, and disappointment followed when it was realized I had the same likes and dislikes as other people. Believe me, an athlete hates that pedestal. It takes life away from simplicity into the field of unreality; so much so that you almost wish you could become a hermit. Anyway, that's how I first regarded Derek—as an ethereal athlete.

I have long since appreciated how I should have respected Derek —for the hard work and sacrifices he had made to achieve success. This applies to everything in life. As many people who read this book will realize, nothing is gained except by honest endeavour. It is not my object to blow the trumpet of the athlete but merely outline the hard work and sacrifices which must be accepted. I cannot stress too much that if a youngster sets his mind to a goal with an iron determination and is prepared to accept the toil as an opportunity to show his manliness, and his courage, then he must succeed. How many times has this been said in different forms? At first I doubted it, but now I know it is the stark truth.

History is littered with examples of doubt being the downfall of man, even a nation, and often an athlete. But doubt always brings an abrupt stop to that complacent, self-satisfied feeling, that there is nothing to worry about. Doubt can sometimes also be a monster in the mind of an athlete. He begins to lose faith in himself.

It is right that an athlete should recognize his weaknesses, but he should not allow them to overpower him. This is illustrated by those who possess confidence in themselves. They have learned to control the doubt.

Then, of course, comes the physical hardship. There are many athletes who never really know the pain of a hard solid run, and yet it is one of the most cleansing things that can be experienced— the wonderful knowledge of knowing that sometimes the weak body can be mastered.

As in all things which are done frequently, the element of drudgery comes in. This associated with the pain of hard training is probably the main cause for men leaving competitive athletics when they have reached some measure of success, but have by no means tapped the full reservoir of their ability.

Yes, Derek, if I had experienced and known these things when you broke the world mile record, I would have respected you in a far different and more real sense than perhaps I did at the time. You did a Man's job for yourself and country.

Anyway, I followed along a path similar to Derek's and arrived in England to compete in the British Empire Games. During the two or three weeks before the Games a number of athletics events were arranged for the mutual benefit of the British and Empire athletes. It was at the 1958 A.A.A. Championships I first met Derek and Terry O'Connor, and I also had time to be convincingly beaten by Brian Hewson and Mike Rawson in a half-mile. Quite a busy afternoon and a day I shall always remember.

I suppose I met Derek suspiciously because he was a rival. But within a few minutes this 'bloke' had me convinced he wasn't too bad. It is always interesting to meet a champion—to try and determine his qualities.

We were later to meet on many occasions. I found on training with Derek that he had a very competitive spirit. This spirit is a birthright. It is what makes us grit our teeth instead of giving in when someone tries to beat us to the tape. It is the hallmark of a champion.

I stayed with Derek and his lovely wife Madeleine and enjoyed every moment. Madeleine was a world-class half-miler before marrying, and I have no hesitation in saying her unselfishness and understanding were a great boost to Derek on his path to greatness. And as I write this foreword I feel it is for *their* book.

So, in quick reckoning, I think Derek's greatness comes from his competitive spirit; the will to excel; strength built into him from years of hard cross-country running; and the accompanying ability to drive himself to the limits of endurance.

But there are thousands of things which go together to make a champion, and for each one they are different. Derek is a champion of England and the world as an athlete and a man. He had the qualities to get there and did the work necessary. Bravo Derek, bravo Madeleine.

Derek refused to recognize any achievement as the 'summit', and I, too, spend no time pondering on the limit of the mile. The times will become faster and 3 min. 50 sec. will be bettered. As for the ultimate limit your guess is as good as mine.

Don't forget, if we really wish to attain a goal and do all in our power to get it, it will be reached. For success, don't use other people as a criterion. The criterion is: 'Have I done my best?'

Introduction

Since I was a child I have been running into trouble. There have been triumphs and disappointments. In those early days there were no complications in my sporting career. I ran because I possessed a natural ability to beat others and this compensated for my failure to make the school football or cricket teams.

As success breeds ambition my targets grew with my ability. First I wanted to be the best boy at school. Then my boundaries were extended to other schools and eventually Huddersfield. After this I turned to my native county of Yorkshire. When I became a county champion it was only natural I should seek a national title. Finally there was only the world left to conquer. At this stage my career interested thousands of people whom I did not know. I was not alone when I won and lost. Eventually I achieved my boyhood ambition on a July evening in 1957 when I broke the world mile record.

In the moment of victory I did not realize that the inner force, which had been driving me to my ultimate goal, died when I became the world's fastest miler. My failure to realize this meant that within a year I was yesterday's hero. The headlines no longer called me the golden boy. They criticized. I became the champion who seldom won. Some of the comments were cruel and life lost a lot of its gaiety. My mother, who has been an invalid most of her life, was upset about what was frequently written and we tried to keep certain newspapers away from her. In this book I reveal frankly why I failed.

Criticism from Press and public made me determined to come back. It hurt when strangers approached me in the street and complained they had lost money when I had been beaten in a race. There could be no quick return to favour as it takes months to prepare the body for international track races.

But in 1959 I once more felt the warmth of spectators' cheers.

That was on Whit Monday when I won a two-mile race at the British Games, White City, London. Victory was never sweeter. I not only conquered the pain of honest effort—it is always the same in big races—but I had mastered myself and won back my confidence. Only athletes who have competed in major events can appreciate the punishment which must be accepted as the price of victory. In every race there is a crucial moment when the body wants to quit. Then it needs imagination and mental tenacity to survive the crisis. Otherwise the penalty is defeat.

This develops the character. Consequently few athletes can tolerate small-minded officials and there are many. If a more adult approach was used many of the problems between competitors and administrators need never arise. The sport of track and field is more important than any individual. When this is accepted and selfish moves eliminated, then the rows might end.

I have had a lot of fun in athletics. My running has taken me round the world and provided the opportunity to visit almost every country in Europe. A flight over the Pole to Vancouver; dodging sharks in the Pacific waters near Canton; a barbecue on an Australian beach. Of course it is not always so romantic and the demands of competition and training curb the normal joys of many social activities. Against this there is the elation which comes from supreme fitness.

I would have no story to tell without kind help from many people. They are too numerous to mention now but they are included in the following pages—officials, coaches, athletes, journalists, friends and my family. All have played their part in the Ibbotson story.

My final hope is that others might be inspired to take over the baton from me one day.

I

That glorious 3 min. 57·2 sec.

Derek Ibbotson, the Yorkshire character with the wicked grin of a pirate, legs like steel pistons and leather lungs, proved himself the greatest middle distance runner in the world.—*Frank McGhee, Daily Mirror*

AS A BOY running across the Yorkshire moors I used to make believe that I was possessed of some magical power that made me the fastest man on earth—a modern Mercury. Like Walter Mitty with his dreams, I became so absorbed in my flights of fancy that it was always a bit of a shock to 'wake up' and find there were no wings on my heels—just a pair of rather worn sandals.

As my running improved, those early dreams became real ambitions. I remember the day I trained after reading that Gordon Pirie had beaten the brilliant Russian Vladimir Kuts in Norway, 1956, and at the same time had broken the world 5,000-metre record. Every stride seemed to be taking *me* up to a record. Of course I kept these ambitions to myself for fear of making myself a laughing-stock.

It happened once when I was in the R.A.F. in 1955; the other lads in my hut, Y46—yes, I even remember the number—heard I was running against Gordon Pirie and John Disley, both Olympic athletes. They ribbed me and said I was only asked to make the number up. I suppose they were right, but it did not seem that way to me. During that previous winter I had trained seriously for the first time in my life, thanks to the facilities made available by the R.A.F. I did not win that race but it turned out to be the turning-point of my athletic career.

But first I would like to tell you about the race that changed my whole world. It happened on the Friday evening of July 19th,

1957, at the White City. As I glanced round the stadium, I wondered whether any of those friends from Hut Y46 were among the sea of faces in the vast stands.

There was a tense expectancy among the vast crowd. At 8 p.m. I was due to run in the Invitation Mile during the London–New York match against the finest field of middle-distance runners ever assembled up to that time on one track outside the Olympic Games. Many people had forecast that this should be the greatest mile in British athletic history.

I was brimful of confidence, especially jaunty because five weeks earlier my wife Madeleine had presented me with a daughter, Christine, and on the same day I had broken the British and European mile records with a time of 3 min. 58·4 sec. at Glasgow. A week previously at the White City I had beaten the British three-mile record in heavy rain with 13 min. 20·8 sec. Ironically, the day before I had failed to qualify for the A.A.A. mile final.

On the morning of the White City event I had travelled down from Huddersfield where I was working, and was delighted to learn that the organizers had arranged to bring my wife and baby daughter to a London hotel from Hanworth in Middlesex, where they were living at the time. The previous week the trip to Hanworth had caused me to arrive late at the stadium and I had had no time to warm up before my mile heat.

Madeleine and I did not discuss the race, we talked only about the plans I had just received for our new bungalow in Huddersfield. Gooing and clucking at Christine helped me to relax and forget about running, sweat and cinders. A game of golf the previous Tuesday had left me with a stiffness in my right leg, but this was soon forgotten under the spell of Christine's joyful gurgling.

Madeleine naturally wanted to see the meeting—she had represented Britain in the 800 metres—so we took Christine in a carry-cot to the White City, arriving at the stadium an hour before the race. Madeleine had a seat in the restaurant and Christine was fast asleep.

I changed, warmed up, looking for the men I was due to meet. The first rival I saw was the blond Czech, Stanislav Jungwirth, who a week before had run the world's fastest 1,500 metres in the fabulous time of 3 min. 38·4 sec. There is no accurate method of conversion but I estimated that this time was worth around 3 min.

57 sec. for the mile. That was what I was secretly hoping to do myself as the world record stood at 3 min. 58 sec. in the name of John Landy, of Australia, who had retired.

Jungwirth had been competing in top athletics much longer than myself, but was still young. His running style is rather ugly—like a crab movement, with his arms rotating across the body. As he darted up and down in his blue track-suit, I noticed he did not get up on his toes. This made me feel more confident.

Then there was the man in green—Ronnie Delany, from Ireland, who had won the Olympic 1,500 metres at Melbourne the previous year. I have always regretted I was not selected to compete in that race. Ronnie and myself were old friends as we had had long talks during the Melbourne Olympic Games. He was one of many people who tried to entice me to take an athletic scholarship and attend an American university.

Delany is a brilliant runner, and relies mainly on a sprinter's finish to win his races. At the Olympic Games he came through from eighth position to win decisively. Our names had been linked in a controversy in the 1957 season because we had not met in Dublin. I had accepted an invitation to run with a small British team in that lovely city, but had forgotten that I had earlier agreed to compete in Darlington!

This made many people say I was scared to face Ronnie, whereas in fact there was nothing I wanted more. When I heard he was competing in the Invitation Mile, I was delighted, because it meant victory would be more worth while. The only other time I had run against him I had won. That was in the previous year when I first broke the four-minute mile and equalled Roger Bannister's English record. Ronnie was not at his best in that race, but even so it gave me a psychological advantage.

I don't suffer from pre-race anxiety, while Delany is inclined to get keyed up. Some say that this is to my disadvantage, but I have always considered it more sensible to concentrate on trying to analyse the weaknesses of opponents. In the case of Delany I could only hope that the early pace would be so fast that the sting would be taken out of what the Americans had called his 'blow-torch' finish.

Another leading competitor was the Polish champion, Stefan Lewandowski. We had met in Budapest in 1955, and have since

B

become good friends. His record included a number of fast 800-, 1,000- and 1,500-metre times, though I doubted whether he would be good enough over the mile. Many Continentals find the extra 119 yards on top of the 1,500 metres tough going. British sprinters suffer in the same way in the 100 metres as compared with the 100 yards, which is nearly ten yards less.

Then there was Alan Gordon from Oxford University, which has produced such men as Jack Lovelock, Roger Bannister and Chris Chataway. Gordon held the Inter-Varsity Mile record in 4 min. 6·4 sec. I had never had reason to fear Alan over a mile, and I did not think this was the time to start.

One British runner I respected tremendously was Ken Wood, a fellow-Yorkshireman. We had been running against each other since we were kids. The first time I met him was in a two-mile race at Roundhay Park, Leeds. I had taken a thirty-yard lead, and was coasting comfortably round the last lap when my brother shouted out, 'Get moving!' I turned and saw Wood flying towards me. I started to sprint but it was too late. He won. That was our first meeting and it taught me a lesson.

Ken had competed in only one race during the summer. He had trained hard, but that is no replacement for actual racing. It was the same with Chris Chataway, one of my greatest rivals, who caught stomach cramp in the middle of the Olympic 5,000 metres at Melbourne. He had put in a fantastic amount of training just before the Games, but too little competitive running let him down in the last and most important race of his career. Then there was Mike Blagrove, a promising athlete from Ealing Harriers, who had run some fast half-miles. Now, like so many other British athletes, he had been caught by the magic of the mile. Someone suggested to me that Mike might be prepared to lead in the earlier part of the race. This would prove helpful because it would allow me to operate the better of my two plans.

I had sketched out my tactics on the train coming to London that day. If the early pace was fast, I planned to take either second or third position and sprint the final 300 yards. By this method I thought I might break away from Delany, who prefers to leave his strike until the last 120 yards. He had a faster finish than me, and it would be fatal to fight it out on level terms over the last 100 yards. I had to win before this.

If no one was prepared to take the early lead, I decided to go it alone and run the first lap in around 59 seconds, and then step aside for someone else to take over. This plan was less likely to produce a fast time because valuable seconds might be wasted waiting for a new leader. Also, if there was no natural front runner, it could cause a hold-up at the first bend with everyone waiting for the other to take the frontal position.

That will always be one of the difficulties when there are a number of class runners in a mile race. I have never considered this classic distance should be reduced to an all-out sprint over the last lap. The object is surely to prove who is the fastest man over a mile, not 440 yards.

It is also unfair to expect one runner to set the pace throughout for others as he is more likely to be beaten in the rush for the tape. This had happened to me earlier in 1957 when I ran in the U.S.A. After leading all the way I was beaten into fourth place by the Australian, Merv Lincoln. Yet the next day I sat on Lincoln's tail until the last lap and won.

So when I approached Mike Blagrove, I was thinking of the race and not merely of myself.

'Mike, do you think you could step up the first stage of the race?' I asked, as we were warming up twenty minutes before the start.

'Certainly. What time would you like for the half-mile?' he answered.

'I think about one minute fifty-six or one minute fifty-seven seconds. Thanks, Mike.'

Although there were numerous Olympic champions competing at the meeting, the mile was expected to be *the* race. Before the start a roller went round the inside of the track which had been affected by heavy rain that afternoon. The runners were introduced individually to the crowd of 30,000. This is the normal Continental custom, but seldom seen in Britain. I think it adds to the drama of the contest.

Everyone in the race was on edge. Maybe it was because we knew the spectators, television viewers and the world's Press were expecting something sensational. As usual, the stadium seemed a lonely place. I sensed a stern determination amongst the other competitors. Smiles had given way to taut, dedicated expressions.

Delany was drawn on the inside lane and I was next to him. On my right was the tall Lewandowski, then Jungwirth, Blagrove, Wood and Gordon.

The gun cracked, and Blagrove shot off like a hare with the pack after him. In my anxiety to get into a leading position, I brushed past Delany. I muttered, 'Sorry, Ron,' and they were the only words I uttered during the race.

Delany was not in a hurry as he prefers to make his bid from well behind to avoid the early bumping. Thanks to Blagrove the start was fast, and there was no bunching at the first bend. Jungwirth had taken second place, and I was third. This was a good position as the field filed round the bend into the first full straight.

I was running behind Jungwirth for the first time, and his style looked even more awkward. He seemed to shuffle along but there was no wasted effort in his leg action.

The pace was really fierce as we tore down the back-straight, but I was happy. So far everything had gone as I had planned with sports writer Terry O'Connor, who had organized the race on behalf of the London *Evening News* and London clubs. He had studied Jungwirth's great 1,500-metre run a week earlier, and assured me the Czech would follow a fast leader.

At the start of a race it is possible to hear the spectators. There were shouts of: 'Come on, Yorkshire' . . . 'Up, Huddersfield' . . . 'Good old Derek'. . . . It was like stirring music to me, but gradually it faded from my ears as the race progressed.

There was no slackening off in speed as we entered the next bend, and I thought how ridiculous it was that a week earlier on the same track I had failed to qualify for the A.A.A. mile final, and could only run 4 min. 15·5 sec. Now I was moving like a sprinter.

The tiny Blagrove was still in the lead as the field swept past the post for the first lap in the time of 55·3 seconds. On hearing this time, my mind became swamped with figures. Only a couple of times before had I run a faster 440 yards. What would happen if we kept this rate up throughout . . . a mile in 3 min. 40 sec. It was frightening just thinking about it. But then I like working out mathematical problems when running. When I was at technical school I used to unravel mental sums like 14×16 just to occupy the time and help to forget the physical strain and even boredom of running.

Pounding over the heavy track, I could hear the other runners shuffling for new positions behind me. This gave me little concern. The mile event is like a game of poker—you never reveal your hand until the end. I knew Delany, Wood and Lewandowski were on my trail, but there was nothing I could do at this stage. There was still almost three-quarters of the race to go.

Going down the back-straight for the second time, I felt the pace slacken a little. This was a good thing because my legs and arms were already beginning to feel tired, although my breathing was still controlled.

As Jungwirth ran, his feet flicked up cinders which sprayed my legs, giving me a burning sensation which was not unpleasant. I had to be careful not to get spiked. It had happened to me many times before. To prove to myself I was running confidently, I winked at Thelma Hopkins, the British Olympic high-jumper, who was standing on the grass inside the track.

Constant training makes a runner's body hyper-sensitive and any slight difference in race pace registers. That is why I was not surprised when I heard the half-mile time was 1 min. 55·8 sec. We passed the mark still in the same order. Blagrove was right on the target so we still had plenty in hand for a mile in under four minutes.

I was now feeling very tired, but convinced the others felt the same. Yet Jungwirth looked tremendously strong, and seemed as if he could go on indefinitely. We were now in the third lap where so many mile races are decided. I knew Blagrove could not last much longer as his best previous mile was around 4 min. 7 sec., and the psychological strain of running in front of such a pack of runners must soon tell.

What would happen when Blagrove eventually cracked? If Jungwirth was in second place he should be forced to take the lead. I prayed this would be so. This was not the time for me to take over. I had to relax and conserve energy.

The race had become slower over the third lap until it seemed almost a jog. Life was flowing back into my limbs. The feeling filled me with exhilaration and confidence. In front I noticed that Jungwirth was hesitating. He had realized Blagrove could no longer maintain the lead, and had moved up to the little Englishman's shoulders. There was no resistance and the Czech went ahead. Immediately I moved up with him.

Now the pattern of the race was clear. I was going to be able to stake everything on the last lap. Concentrating on the tactics I had already decided, my running became mechanical. Approaching the three-quarter-mile mark, I glanced across the track to the spot where I was to make my bid for victory—300 yards from the tape. I could think of nothing else and was impatient to get there.

As the bell tolled for the last lap, there was a lot of noise and juggling for positions behind me. Everyone was making his own preparation for victory. Any moment now I expected to find someone at my shoulder. Little wonder I did not hear the three-quarter-mile time. I discovered later it was exactly three minutes. But at this stage—locked in a battle for supremacy—records did not matter. Winning was the only thing which counted.

It was vital not to lose my position. Wood was the man I feared at this stage of the race. He had often won the mile with a long-sustained sprint from the bell. Len Kilby, the Olympic masseur, was standing inside the track waving me on frantically, and I felt danger was near. When I found myself still unchallenged with Jungwirth in front at the first bend, I guessed that Wood was still not racing-fit. At the same time I decided it was foolish to worry about the others. I had to concentrate on winning.

It was a strain resisting the temptation to go immediately to the front, but even at this critical moment I did not forget the elementary tactics—never pass on the bend.

'Relax and concentrate on your legs and arms, you are on the brink of your greatest athletic victory, but all will be lost if you lose control,' I counselled myself.

Now the moment of action had arrived. I moved up to Jungwirth, just to test him at first. He held me off. Should I wait or go now? The decision was made for me. Out of the corner of my right eye I caught a glimpse of the Pole, Lewandowski, moving up. Delany and Wood could not be far behind. It was the moment of truth. Fear gave me wings like the Mercury I used to dream of on the Yorkshire moors. I drove past Jungwirth, and was out on my own.

Everything seemed to explode inside me at once. My target was now the end of the final long-straight. I must get there first because no one was likely to challenge at the bend. The crowd was roaring but to me it was just a bizarre rumble like the sound of a distant sea. I was hurtling through a tunnel towards a shimmering light, with wolves snapping at my heels.

As I swung out of the final bend, there were only about sixty yards left. The blood seemed to be draining from my leaden legs. Could I hang on? I was haunted by the ghost of Delany. Was he at my shoulder? With these fears flashing through my mind, I caught an imaginary glimpse of Chris Brasher, the Olympic steeple-chase champion. He had so often been standing in that spot when I raced against Chris Chataway, shouting, 'Relax, Chris,' and although Brasher was not there this time, I seized the message: 'Relax, Derek. . . . Relax, Derek. . . .'

My body ached, I seemed to be suffocating, sweat blurred my vision. I wanted a rival to join me so that I could prove whether I had any energy left to fight.

Ahead was the thin white tape—the respite from the agony. For one horrifying moment it seemed to move away—instead of coming nearer. But the next moment it came towards me, as if a foot wide. I lunged forward—and the victory was real, Mercury could keep his wings.

Elation swept through my body as I brushed away the tape and stepped through the blinding flash of cameras.

I had beaten the Olympic champion, the world's fastest 1,500-metre runner, in a new world record time of 3 min. 57·2 sec.

2

Press comments on the mile

This was the greatest race I have ever seen in my life.—
*Pincus Sober, Chairman of the Foreign Relations Committee
of the Amateur Athletic Union, U.S.A.*

M Y MILE victory at the White City received world-wide
acclaim, and for many weeks I was fêted more like a film
star or pop singer than an amateur runner. Whenever I
appeared there were photographers and reporters. Complete
strangers would speak to me, and most of them believed I would
now become a wealthy man. Little did they know of the stringent
laws associated with amateur athletics.

Of course, I know most of the sports writers who report athletics
and many are my friends. These journalists can, and usually do,
give young sportsmen a lot of help. I have discovered it is much
more difficult to please the critics when you are on top. Some are
downright cruel to those who falter. I will write about this later
because after the mile everyone was so kind. Maybe too kind!

Roger Bannister, whose name has become immortalized as
the first man to break the four-minute-mile barrier, wrote in the
Sunday Times: 'Last Friday's mile came as near to perfection as a
mile can. A race with only two great runners pitched against each
other is always in danger of becoming a farce. Each eyes the other,
both are reluctant to lead, and the race is often won on the finishing
straight in a slow time.

'From the spectator's point of view, three runners are a guarantee
against disappointment, for one runner is unlikely to fool two
opponents and win after a dawdle. The question in every mind on
Friday night was "Who will lead?" Not Ibbotson, for he met his

24

worst defeat at the hands of Lincoln in Los Angeles last May by leading from the gun. Afterwards he vowed he would never lead again. Not Delany, for he is the master of many close finishes, including the Olympic 1,500 metres final in which he sauntered to the front with an almost nonchalant confidence. Not Jungwirth, for he is a half-miler to be feared and the world record holder for 1,500 metres at 3 min. 38·1 sec. which he set up only a week ago.

'So Friday's race could have ended in anti-climax. It was saved by the unselfish running of Michael Blagrove, of Ealing Harriers. A 4 min. 7 sec. miler, he could not hope to win, but at Ibbotson's request he carried three of the greatest milers in the world through their greatest stages of anxiety.

'The first lap was too fast to be ideal (55·3 sec.), the half in 1 min. 55·8 sec. was as fast as in any sub-four-minute mile. A record seemed likely. When Blagrove suddenly faded after two and a half laps at this unaccustomed pace, his work had been done. The speed sagged in the third lap to 64·2 sec.—uneconomically slow. At this point the perfect foundations so carefully laid might have collapsed if these three great runners had feared one another too much and failed to do battle.

'To everyone's delight, Jungwirth kept the field moving and striding steadily, with his arms awkwardly held in an egg-and-spoon race fashion, he passed the bell in exactly three minutes, a shade slower than we had hoped but still making a unique time possible. Ibbotson was second with Lewandowski, the Polish champion, third. After ten yards of the back-straight, Ibbotson moved up to Jungwirth's shoulder. It was not a decisive crushing sprint, but rather a hesitating drawing level as though he doubted the wisdom of leading with two hundred yards to go, and Delany still lurking behind him. Yet by the last bend Ibbotson was in full command of the race, with Lewandowski in second position and Delany just beyond the range of one of his finishing rushes. Ibbotson never faltered for a stride—it was his usual flamboyant performance to the tape.

'The paradox for Derek Ibbotson is this. Because of the uneven running in this mile he is at this moment capable of a time of 3 min. 55 sec. Every runner has a range of events at which he can excel, Ibbotson has never run a fast half-mile in his life and a mile is his shortest event. His style and stride are more that of a two-miler, and one hardly dares to estimate his potential at this, his best distance. Ibbotson can certainly set up a new world record at the upper limit of his running range on the track, three miles or 5,000 metres, and could vanquish the Russian Kuts.'

Frank McGhee, Daily Mirror : 'At last they were lined up. The fair-haired Ibbotson in his powder-blue vest, the colour of the summer sky. The gaunt, dark-haired Delany, Olympic Gold Medallist. Red-shirted, blond-haired Jungwirth, world record holder for 1,500 metres. These were the men we knew we had to watch. But it wasn't one of them who sprang into the lead. It was chunky Mike Blagrove of Britain, with Jungwirth breathing down his neck, Ibbotson third and Delany fourth. That's how they stayed all through the first lap, run at a fantastic speed of 55·3 sec. I was worried. I found myself worrying out loud, "It's too fast; it's too fast."

'This was the pace that kills. I found out afterwards that Ibbotson thought so too. The order stayed the same at the half-mile, with the second lap covered in a more reasonable 60·5 sec. Then Blagrove, his job well done, brilliantly done, relaxed, and in the back-straight the field started to overtake him as though he were standing still. Yet it was a slow third lap, for a three-quarter-mile time of 3 min. exactly. As the bell went for the last lap, the order was Jungwirth, Ibbotson, Lewandowski the Pole, Alan Gordon of Britain, Delany, Wood. But then we had eyes only for Ibbotson as he moved outside Jungwirth, challenging him, drew level and then went away. Faster, faster, gloriously faster he ran, to come in alone, twelve yards in front of Delany—the danger man. Delany's famous blow-torch finishing sprint failed him. Or, rather, the searing, white-hot pace had burnt it out of him.'

Roy Moor, News Chronicle : 'Expectations ran high amidst the tense crowd. Suddenly, with three hundred yards to go, Ibbotson challenged Jungwirth for the lead. He got it and then went careering away from the Czech. Rallying his strength, Jungwirth went in hot pursuit of the Yorkshireman. So did Delany. So did Wood, to our surprise, and the Pole, Lewandowski. Only momentarily, however, could they make an impression. Tearing round the final bend as if his heels bore wings, Ibbotson came storming into the straight a good eight yards up on Jungwirth.'

Harry Carpenter, Daily Mail: 'Landy's record was menaced from the crack of the gun, as up to the front went minor hero Mike Blagrove to sacrifice himself at a killing pace. Trailing him came the blond Jungwirth, then Ibbotson, barrel chest thrust out, shadowed by the tall figure of Delany, the Olympic 1,500 metres champion. It was the same order at the half-mile, but Blagrove was done, his mission completed. He fell back; eventually dropped out altogether. His part in this epic race must never be forgotten. Jungwirth, a born front runner, willingly took over. The first big shake-up came as Lewandowski, a handsome, long-legged Pole, moved up past Delany to third place.

'They swept round the bell . . . time three minutes exactly. Nothing could prevent a four-minute mile now. On the back-straight, opposite the finishing line, Ibbotson pounced. He surged past Jungwirth. Two hundred yards to go. Where was Delany, the man with the blow-torch finish? Into the bend for the last time, nobody could catch Ibbotson now as he streaked for home, seeming to gain strength from every stride. You needed three eyes. One on Ibbotson, one on the hands of the giant scoreboard clock as it ticked remorselessly towards the four-minute mark, and one on Delany.'

Laurie Pignon, Daily Sketch: 'Derek Ibbotson, twenty-five-year-old Yorkshireman, parked his wife and month-old baby at London's White City, and went out on to the track to win a world record mile in a million. Ten million people watching on TV and a wonder-struck crowd of 30,000 in the stadium saw the grinning Yorkshireman break John Landy's record.'

Frank Rostron, Daily Express: 'The marvel of it all was that this laughing jester of the world's running tracks finished so fresh.

'It was a blood-tingling race right from the bell, at a blistering pace that immediately made a world record certain. But Ibbotson's irresistibly strong finish and comparatively simple win robbed the race of the expected drama.

'Blagrove, a half-miler, came in at the last minute in the role of a pace-maker. He carried out instructions to prevent a tactical dawdle by the assembled squadron of flyers. But Ibbotson's superb condition made it seem he would have won however the race had been run.

'Round the final bend came Ibbotson's pounding unfaltering legs. Increasing his lead with every stride. He was at least six yards clear as, head proudly high and knees rising like pistons, he propelled himself unwaveringly to the tape.'

The Times Athletics Correspondent (*Neil Allen*) *:* 'It was the first time that four men have ever beaten four minutes in a race, but much more important, Ibbotson's victory was the greatest in modern middle-distance running, surpassing even R. G. Bannister's defeat of John Landy in 1954. Ibbotson had defeated Delany, the Olympic 1,500-metre champion, Jungwirth, the 1,500-metre world record holder, and the clock. No one could ask more.'

Describing the last lap, *The Times* correspondent wrote: 'Then came the kill. After five yards of the last back-straight Ibbotson came up to Jungwirth's shoulder, seemed to ponder his risky position for a fraction and then was off, striding away with Jungwirth struggling. It was a frighteningly early stage at which to strike with such a field behind him, but it was a gamble worth taking for Ibbotson, as an international three-miler, had more stamina than any of his rivals. Round the final bend he charged with Lewandowski now ahead of Jungwirth and still in contention until the final straight was reached. It seemed all over, but not before Delany had come rushing past Lewandowski and Jungwirth on the last bend, giving us just as shiver at a suggestion of the great finish which won him his title at Melbourne.'

Terry O'Connor, Evening News: 'Ibbotson is now monarch of the mile. Behind his enthronement is a fascinating story. I was always convinced this remarkable athlete was capable of breaking the record. Three years ago when I first saw him run, I knew he was a future world champion. He has the qualities which make kings of sport—physical ability, spirit and mental mastery.

'When an invitation mile was first arranged in this spectacular meeting, I talked with Ibbotson about a new world record. On the day of the race we discussed tactics, and he agreed a fierce opening pace was necessary to ensure Ron Delany, the Irish Olympic champion, could not exploit his excellent finish.'

I would like to end with the comments of the two men I feared most in the race—Ron Delany and Stanislav Jungwirth.

Delany: 'It was a fabulous race, and a pleasure as well as a privilege to run it. I shall dream about it for years.'

Jungwirth: 'I was disappointed that I did not add the world mile record to my 1,500 metres' record time, but I think Ibbotson was a deserved and good winner, and I am looking forward to meeting him again.'

3

Is the record mine?

Fastest man on feet, the four-minute miler, Derek Ibbotson, wins the *Daily Sketch* Sports Popularity Poll in a gallop. Three times in 1957 Derek smashed his way through the lung-splitting four-minute barrier. Climax was the mile in a million at the red-hot White City in July, which he won in the world record time of 3 min. 57·2 sec.—*Laurie Pignon, Daily Sketch*

WITH the race over, I could hear the crowd's roar properly for the first time. It was as if I had been deaf and my hearing had returned. As I waited for Delany and the other runners I glanced up at the giant minute clock, and saw that the hand had stopped just short of four minutes. It looked like 3 min. 57 sec., but you can never be sure. A fraction of a second can make the difference between beating a record or failing.

I was now shaking hands with Ron Delany who said, 'It was a dream of a race,' before moving away to the rails, convulsed in pain. Ron is a highly strung athlete who burns up nervous energy in a race. This means he suffers before and afterwards.

After Delany the other competitors came in, Jungwirth, Wood, Lewandowski, and finally Gordon. While I was shaking hands, Jack Crump, then British athletics team manager, dashed up and congratulated me, and said I had broken the world record. The significance of this did not register until the stadium became hushed for an announcement over the tannoy system.

'Winner of the Invitation Mile was No. 71, G. D. Ibbotson, of Great Britain, in a time which, subject to ratification, is a new ground, English Native, British National, British All-Comers, European and World record of 3 min. . . . .' The announcer's clinical voice was drowned by a new explosion of cheers.

I doubt whether many people heard the remaining figures '57·2 seconds'. A British victory and a world record was all the spectators wanted. Immediately after the announcement I was aware of a glowing feeling inside me. I had achieved a boyhood dream. This was the greatest moment of my life, and I naturally did not realize at the time the frustration which was to follow because of those three words *subject to ratification*.

Still in my track-suit I was interviewed by television, the Press and radio. The sports writers asked me questions about the race for some twenty minutes, and I answered them honestly. This has often got me into trouble, but that is how I was brought up in Yorkshire.

You will come to no harm if you tell the truth! How often I was told that when I was a child, but now I wonder whether it is always so.

'Was there any plan, Derek?' asked the *Daily Sketch* correspondent.

'Only to try and run faster than my rivals.'

'What about Mike Blagrove?' queried the *Daily Herald* man.

'Just before the race I asked Mike whether he was prepared to make the early pace to avoid a stalemate, with everyone watching everyone else. He jumped at the idea and I was very grateful to him.'

After all the interviews I went to look in the restaurant for my wife Madeleine. Little Christine was still asleep under a table where she had been throughout the race. Madeleine and I drank champagne with the Marquis of Exeter—formerly Lord Burghley, the Olympic hurdles champion—and Mr. C. R. Willis, Editor of the London *Evening News*. It was truly a champagne evening because Clive Adams, of British European Airways, presented me with three bottles. He had promised one for every second under four minutes. I did not quibble about the odd fifth of a second!

There was little time to continue the celebrations as I had to catch a night train to Newcastle where I had promised to run the next day. That night I never slept. All the time I was re-running the race in my mind. Next day the newspapers were full of the mile record. But there was no mention of pace-making. That blew up a few days later.

Before I tell you of the incidents that followed, let me quote the

International Amateur Athletic Federation's law on pace-making:
'*In deciding whether the competition was a bona fide one the International Amateur Athletic Federation will consider whether the claimant was unfairly assisted towards the time accomplished by pacing from another competitor apparently designed to assist him to achieve a record.*'

It is also important to point out there was an international jury at the meeting. They included the Marquis of Exeter, President of the I.A.A.F., Mr. Pincus Sober and Jack Crump. Also my mile record form was signed by the following prominent officials, J. C. Crump, Secretary of the British Amateur Athletic Board, E. H. L. Clynes, Secretary of the Amateur Athletic Association, A. D. Thwaites, Treasurer of the A.A.A., Les. Truelove, then A.A.A. Team Manager, Pincus Sober, Chairman of the Foreign Relations Committee of the Amateur Athletic Union, U.S.A., and W. Morton, Irish International Athletic Official.

Now I will tell you the reasons given why the record should not be passed. It appears Walter Jewell, a former Treasurer of the A.A.A., was asked to sign the record form but declined. Some days after the race he gave an interview to the *News Chronicle*, stating his views for this action. They read as follows:

'Critics of my refusal to sign the application for Ibbotson's run of 3 min. 57·2 sec. to be ratified as a world record seem to overlook a very important point. International rules *now* do not permit the record-breaker to have the assistance of a pace-maker. Our own officials should be fully aware of this, for it was the British Board's recommendation which the I.A.A.F. approved when unanimously agreeing to ban paced races from record acceptance at the Congress in Melbourne in 1956.

'Although this and other important changes were adopted and properly advised to the delegates of the A.A.A. General Committee, few appear to have taken the trouble to read and study the reports.

'I am not hostile to Derek Ibbotson. On the contrary, I have been able to offer him advice on several occasions—it has been appreciated.

'Paced races are either banned from record-making or they are not. There can be no half-way measures. As the I.A.A.F. say they are banned I would be failing in my duty as an official of the

Mike Blagrove (77), the man who caused the 'pace-making' furore, leads Stanislav Jungwirth, Ibbotson and Ronnie Delany at the end of the first lap of Ibbotson's world-record mile at the White City, July 19th, 1957

Right: End of the agony, beginning of the glory—Ibbotson breasts the tape and the watches show 3 min. 57·2 sec., beating John Landy's world record by four-fifths of a second

Below: Success is so sweet—Ibbotson receives his prize from the Marquess of Exeter after his world-record mile. The Marquess, formerly Lord Burghley, is a former Olympic champion

A.A.A. if I recommended for recognition as a record a run which I considered was aided by a pace-maker.'

Mr. Jewell was also quoted as saying: 'In the light of Ibbotson's statement, reported after the event, there was little doubt in my mind that it falls within the category of our earlier discussion. If somebody's indiscretion has been allowed to overflow, there is not much we as officials of the governing association can do about it.'

I take this last statement to mean that if I had not given any credit to Blagrove, there would have been no controversy. Is this the penalty for honesty? Yet I had made it clear after the race that Blagrove was not trying to help *me* achieve a record, but ensure this much-boosted event did not become a farcical dawdle. In the previous chapter Roger Bannister pointed out that the mile might have been an anti-climax but for the unselfish running of Blagrove.

If Jungwirth or Delany had won, would there have been the same fuss? I doubt it because neither spoke to Blagrove, yet they enjoyed the same advantages. If gambling existed in athletics—I am glad it is prohibited—I consider Delany and Jungwirth would both have been favoured above me. When there was only a lap left, five men were bunched together and Blagrove had already dropped out, so he could no longer influence the result. To prove how close was the finish just look at the detailed result.

1. Derek Ibbotson   3 min. 57·2 sec.
2. Ron Delany   3 min. 58·8 sec.
3. Stanislav Jungwirth   3 min. 59·1 sec.
4. Ken Wood   3 min. 59·3 sec.
5. Stefan Lewandowski   4 min. 0·6 sec.
6. Alan Gordon   4 min. 3·4 sec.

Four men eclipsed the once-formidable four-minute barrier, and it was still suggested that the race was arranged for me to break the world record. Strangely, there was no fuss when I broke the British and European mile times at Glasgow earlier in the season. Yet in this case I had more advantageous pace-making than at the White City. Les Locke and Paul Soine (South Africa) both helped by sharing the first two laps in a fast time. Then I took over and completed the mile in 3 min. 58·4 sec.

C

The only argument I can remember then was about the track, as it is slightly banked at the bends as in Malmö, Sweden.

Fortunately, it did not matter because the inside lanes are flat. It is strange these discrepancies only seem to be discovered when there is a record. The creation of new times is the life-blood of the sport, but when they happen there always seems to be a move by someone to prevent the time being recognized.

The pace-making law has changed twice since the war. When Sydney Wooderson set up his world mile record at Motspur Park in 1937, he was helped by a relay of runners to create a new time of 4 min. 6·4 sec. After the war the law was changed to prevent records being established during handicap-type races.

Then in 1954 Roger Bannister created history by becoming the first man to run a mile in under four minutes. This was a carefully planned 'race' with Chris Brasher, later to win an Olympic gold medal, and my old rival, Chris Chataway, setting the pace for three-and-a-half laps. Brasher led for the first half-mile, and then Chataway took over for the critical third circuit. He was still leading with less than 300 yards to go, when Bannister went ahead to achieve his time of 3 min. 59·4 sec. This could not be described as a *bona fide* race. It was really a time-trial arranged to break the four-minute mile.

I have a tremendous admiration for Bannister. He dared to tread where others had feared. He broke a psychological barrier which was holding back athletic progress. He put Britain on top of the world, and inspired thousands to follow in his wake.

Yet at the same time it would have had a bad effect on running if such manufactured records became more important than winning a good race. In 1955 the A.A.A. drafted a new law. It is the one I quoted, and now accepted by the world-governing body of athletics. This was designed to prevent a repetition of the Bannister-type of race where only one man was designed to win. Whether it was necessary, I am not sure. Even if you had an electrically controlled figure set to run the mile in under 3 min. 50 sec., that alone could not help a human being to run under that time if he did not have the talent, speed and strength. And, maybe more important, a belief that such a time is possible. There is no mystic formula for athletic success, only hard work. I have discovered this many times.

Unfortunately, the new law has been badly misinterpreted in many circles, so there is a general belief that all pace-making is wrong. This is not so. Only when the sole object is to help an individual set a record. In some races, where there are a number of outstanding runners, it is vital that one of the non-stars sets the early momentum, otherwise it could become a cat-and-mouse affair with everyone watching the other until the last 440 yards. When this happens it is not a true test to prove the best man over a mile.

Of course, it can be said that the best runners should be able to go out in front and grind the opposition into the ground. The most successful exponent of this form of miling was John Landy, the Australian, who took the record from Bannister. And, also, my successor Herb Elliott.

It has been reported that when Landy made his mile time of 3 min. 58 sec. he was paced by Chataway. This is not true. Chataway was very much in the race, but Landy led after the first few hundred yards. Chataway tried to hang on and was still up at the third lap, and more likely acted as a spur to the Australian.

Yet even Landy discovered in the 1954 Empire Games, at Vancouver, when he met Bannister for the first and only time, how difficult it is always to lead, and win against the very best opposition. Bannister allowed Landy to get twelve yards ahead of him in one part of the race so he could run more to his own schedule. But at the start of the last lap, Bannister was back in contact so he would be ready for his final strike.

When I ran in Los Angeles, 1957, against Brian Hewson, Merv Lincoln of Australia and Laszlo Tabori, the Hungarian refugee, I learnt how Landy must have felt in Vancouver. I tried to run the opposition off their feet but they were still pounding at my heels when we came to the half-way stage. This is the time when a runner starts to worry about saving something in reserve for the final lap, and automatically slows down. This is why the majority of the third laps in mile races are slower than the others. But the real truth is you can never keep enough in reserve when holding the lead. No doubt this is mental, as some people suggest, but that's how it seems to me. In Los Angeles I was still in front when there were a hundred and fifty yards left. Around the final bend the race really began. Those who had trailed behind were now fighting for the lead and I was trapped inside as my rivals went past. This was the penalty for acting as pace-maker, and I ended in fourth position, with Lincoln the winner.

The next evening I met Lincoln again in Modesto, California. This time I decided to keep behind the Australian and won easily.

Even the greatest of them all, Herb Elliott, does not attempt to lead until the half-way stage of his big races. When he created world records for the mile and 1,500 metres in 1958, his Australian team-mate, Alby Thomas, helped with the early pace on both occasions. Incidentally, there was no suggestion of illegal tactics then, and I agree. In both races he was up against some of the world's best middle-distance runners. But it does add to the irony of how I suffered to gain recognition.

When the British Amateur Athletic Board accepted my mile time as a new British All-comers record I felt confident that the International Amateur Athletic Federation would follow the same course. Yet when there was a European Congress meeting in 1957, it was decided to defer my record with a few others until the full meeting of the I.A.A.F. in Stockholm the following August during the European Championships. This meant waiting thirteen months after running the race.

By this time Elliott had run a faster mile so it was little consolation to me that my record was accepted without even a discussion. As so often happens, officialdom had moved too slowly.

4

Early days—early races

He began his running career at Almondbury as a schoolboy
showing 'guts' and determination against bigger and older
boys to gain school and cross-country honours.—*Huddersfield
Examiner*

M
Y FIRST race was at the age of five—and, my goodness, how
important it was to me. My mother had taken me to the
infants' school at Berry Brow, where I was born. School
didn't seem so good, so I decided to run home. It was only one
hundred and fifty yards but, with tears streaming down my face, it
felt like a mile.

When I was born, on June 17th, 1932, the world mile record
stood at 4 min. 9·2 sec. in the name of a Frenchman, Jules Ladou-
megue, who was the first man to break the 'barrier' of 4 min.
10 sec. Not that that meant a lot in hilly Berry Brow, where folks
believed in taking their time.

My first interest in athletics came when I used to visit my uncle
Scott Heeley, the local greengrocer, and listened to stories of his
exploits as a harrier. The only part of these reminiscences that I can
remember now is that Uncle Scott finally gave up after being sick
through running too soon after eating steak-and-kidney pie.

My father, a small chubby man who died in 1958, also stimulated
my interest by proudly telling me of Tommy Matthewman, a sprinter
who brought fame to Huddersfield when he represented Britain at
the Olympic Games in 1936.

My mother's sister, who was a good high-jumper, provided the
only other trace of athletic background in the family.

Stuart, my elder brother, would sometimes allow me to accompany
him to the recreation ground where we played football and cricket.

37

In a Yorkshire village, games are always the predominant feature. There was no television and we rarely went to the pictures.

Although I tried hard, I was not a particularly good ball-player. And on the one occasion when I did manage to be selected to play for the school soccer team my father would not give me the money for my bus fare to the match because I had arrived home late.

My family was not well off, and my mother did not enjoy the best of health. She was rather frail, but had tremendous spirit and determination. My parents made many sacrifices to give my brother and myself a good education. But my boyhood was happy. There were so many facilities around Berry Brow for enjoyment. We used to go in parties, scrump in the orchards, build rafts on the river Holme and swim in the reservoir.

When I won a scholarship to Almondbury Grammar School, I surprised my headmaster at the junior school. He always claimed that I was interested only in sport. I was at the grammar school during the war years and one of our favourite pastimes was chasing parachutes. Nearby there was a pyrotechnic works, and as part of their experiments they would fire Very lights into the air. At about two hundred feet the lid of the canister would come off and lights floated down to earth at the end of a parachute. Often they would travel for miles in the wind, and we used to chase them, picking them out of rivers and trees to sell so they could be made into hand-kerchiefs or pillowcases. I suppose certain amateur fanatics might say I used my athletic ability for financial gain! My first pair of running-shorts were made out of this parachute material.

I am sure this type of running bred in me the stamina which was to take me to fame.

At Almondbury Grammar School cross-country running was compulsory every week, and I shall never forget my first race. Only one lad, who had stayed down in the same form from the previous year, knew the course, and he showed the others the way. I kept up with the leaders, and when it came to the last part of the course the older and bigger boy set off on his own. I stayed with him, and managed to take the lead a hundred yards from the finish.

This encouraged me to enter the Junior School Cross-Country Championship (eleven to thirteen years) and I finished fifth. The winner was Jeff Taylor, who later played football for Huddersfield Town, Fulham and Brentford before becoming an operatic singer.

His brother also plays soccer for Huddersfield, and cricket for Yorkshire. In my second attempt at the junior cross-country I was third and eventually won at the age of thirteen.

When, at fourteen, I entered for the senior cross-country, I believed I could win, and was leading at four-and-a-half miles when I took the wrong path and got lost. About twenty of the best runners followed me and we were about half a mile behind when we returned to the course. I did not give up, and eventually caught the new leaders with about four hundred yards to go, but this effort exhausted me and I was beaten by ten yards.

On the Summer Sports Day I used to try all events, but had most success over the 440 yards, 880 yards and mile. The masters encouraged me to enter for the open events around the district, and I found the opposition much tougher. I was often beaten by E. M. Weaving, who was a member of Longwood Harriers. His success gave me the idea of joining a club.

I left school at sixteen, to become an apprentice electrician with the British Electricity Authority at thirty shillings a week. I also delivered newspapers, and was able to buy myself a second-hand bike for thirty shillings. While with the British Electricity Authority I went to the Huddersfield Technical College, and at the age of eighteen qualified for a scholarship to attend full-time at the college, where I took a Higher National Diploma in electrical engineering. My parents went without holidays to make this extra education possible.

I had joined Longwood Harriers, and received a lot of help from Cyril Foster, the club coach who had captained the Army of the Rhine team in Sydney Wooderson's days. About that time I met Len Eyre, who won an Empire Games title in 1950. He gave me some helpful tips on how to get more rhythm in my stride.

I owe a lot to the discipline my father imposed on me. He believed that races were won in bed. If I was home late my pocket money was stopped, which meant missing my run at weekends—a dreaded punishment. As I progressed Dad kept newspaper cuttings and wore my first Yorkshire gold medal on his gold chain. But my mother at first used to worry when I came home tired from training. 'I don't think it will do you any good, you know,' she used to fret. Like Dad she later became keen and my staunch supporter.

When only sixteen I had run at the Longwood Harriers Diamond

Jubilee sports meeting at Huddersfield. Len Eyre gained a mile victory over Doug Wilson in 4 min. 9 sec., and Bill Nankeville won the half-mile in 1 min. 53·4 sec. I felt terribly important competing at the same meeting as such well-known athletes. I took part in a junior match, and won the mile by sixty yards.

Larry Montague reported in the *Manchester Guardian*: 'Most notable among the juniors was a mile by G. D. Ibbotson in 4 min. 30·5 sec. His five laps in 52 sec., 55 sec., 55 sec., 55 sec. and 53·5 sec. were wonderful even for a boy, and in sharp contrast to the junior half-mile winner's two quarters in 58 sec. and 67 sec.'

This was my first milestone. I was not training seriously but men like Sidney Quinn, secretary of Longwood Harriers, Cyril Foster, and the trainer Herbert Boothroyd filled me with enthusiasm and I began to train at home by myself on one or two nights a week. On Saturday the club held a six-mile run which I always enjoyed.

I was just seventeen when the Olympic Games were held in London in 1948, but I couldn't afford to visit Wembley. As we did not have a television set all I saw of the Games was on the newsreels. As I watched the giants like Zatopek, Reiff, Wint, Whitfield, Patton and Dillard I dared to hope that one day I might run in this greatest of sporting tournaments.

At that time I could not aspire higher than local events and I won a number of prizes competing for Longwood Harriers and the local Y.M.C.A. My best achievements were in winning the Yorkshire junior mile three years in succession—1949, 1950, 1951. The next year, as a senior, my scope broadened. A victory over Frank Aaron in the Yorkshire three-miles earned me my first race at the White City, London, in the Inter-Counties Championships. On that occasion Gordon Pirie broke Sydney Wooderson's British record by almost 10 seconds with a time of 13 min. 44·8 sec. However, I was pleased to record my best time so far of 14 min. 6·8 sec. for fifth place. My next big event was the Northern Counties three miles, in which I ran second to Alan Parker, who later reached the Olympic 5,000-metre final at Helsinki in 1952.

By this time I was conjuring up hopes that I might make the Helsinki Olympic Games myself. Whatever faint prospect there might have been ended when my final exams for a Higher National Diploma clashed with the A.A.A. championships.

That was virtually the end of my 1952 season. After my exams I went on a six-week holiday to the south of France. On my return I ran in the Yorkshire six miles and managed to beat thirty minutes, but a new job with the National Coal Board near Barnsley took up most of my time. At Barnsley I tried a little coaching but this upset my own training.

An accident in the coal-mine where I worked sliced 1953 out of my athletic calendar. I tripped over a railway line and twisted an ankle badly. I kept on running but a month afterwards I almost collapsed with pain on the track with my ankle ligaments badly torn. The next six weeks were spent on crutches.

In 1954 I made a come-back but my performances were little better than two years previously. Again I was second in the Northern Championships, this time behind Ken Wood. At the end of the year I joined the R.A.F. and for the first time learned the secrets of track and cross-country training. That proved the end of my gay carefree attitude. Running became a serious business. I gained more successes, but lost a lot of the fun.

5

Warned to stop running

Derek Ibbotson, a powerhouse of human energy if ever
there was one.—*Doug Wilson, News of the World*

'OH DEAR, get a doctor,' said the nurse who took my
pulse rate when I went for an R.A.F. medical in 1954. The
nurse seemed very concerned and a couple of doctors came
over to find out the trouble. They both checked my pulse, and
one asked, 'Do you play any games?'

'I run a little.'

'You must run quite a lot to get a pulse rate of just over forty,'
said one of the doctors.

The nurse had recovered her composure, and sighed. 'I thought
he was dying.'

Medical opinion is divided about the pulse rate of an athlete.
Some doctors believe a low rate is due to heavy training schedules,
while others consider it is a birthright. I support the first theory,
because my own rate has come down considerably in recent years
and has been as low as thirty-eight compared with the normal
seventy-two.

The second theory is intriguing because, if proved, it would
mean one could take the pulse rate of schoolboys and sort out those
who were potentially great middle-distance runners.

Roger Bannister, who applied his medical knowledge when
he was training for the first four-minute mile, says: 'The pulse rate
can vary tremendously, according to a boy's temperament. Also
the pulse is only one facet of a complicated number of measurements which would need to be taken by those attempting to decide
whether a boy could become a top-flight runner.'

Russia and other Communist countries pay great attention to

the medical side of sport. They would very much like to find a medical formula for producing Olympic champions. When the British team went to Moscow for the first time in 1955, Russian doctors selected a number of our athletes, and gave them thorough medical examinations. Their coaches provided statistical data, and no doubt they thought that Russians with the same medical measurements could produce similar performances.

But that immeasurable factor which some call 'spirit' and others 'guts' is often the determining factor in sporting success. Nothing can compensate for the lack of will to fight when the situation demands.

Some runners allow their pulse rate to govern them. I remember Gordon Pirie saying he was not feeling well after he had narrowly lost a mile race. When asked what was wrong, he said, 'I took my pulse rate as usual this morning and found it was forty-one—it is normally thirty-eight, so I cannot be in tip-top condition.'

A runner with a pulse rate of forty has a better chance of producing a fast time over a mile than someone with a rate of seventy-two because there is a greater margin before maximum effort is reached. The heart is the engine, drawing oxygen from the lungs and then pumping blood around the body. Obviously someone who trains continually for a number of years must improve the action of his heart. In time it is transformed from an eight-horse-power engine to a Rolls-Royce. This means that at the end of an athletics career the heart must be more efficient, and could account for so many runners enjoying a longer span of life than others.

Many parents fear that too much exercise might damage the heart. This is baseless. Providing there is nothing organically wrong with the heart, running can only improve it.

I had a shock when I applied for a job as an electrical engineer with the National Coal Board in 1952. After a medical examination, the doctor told me there was something wrong with my heart. He advised me to stop running for a month and then return for another check-up. These were the most unhappy weeks of my life. How near I came to giving up running for good.

When the month was up, I was sent to a specialist in Huddersfield, and told that I had a 'murmur' in my heart. After further tests and X-rays, my heart was passed as organically sound, but I discovered many men were discharged from the Services on full pensions during the 1914–18 war because of a similar 'murmur'. Fortunately, medical science has now discovered that in some cases there is no danger in this condition.

Since breaking the world mile record I have undertaken many medical tests to satisfy the curiosity of the experts. One of the most thorough took place when I was in Finland. At the Department of Physiology, in the University of Turku, John Disley, Derek Johnson and myself were examined to discover our oxygen intake. I had the greatest oxygen intake capacity of all the athletes who had been seen there up to that time. And believe me, I use this capacity to the full.

But my medical worries were not yet over. When I was in Cardiff during the 1958 Empire Games, the English coach, Dennis Watts, thought there was something wrong with my left leg. There was speculation as to whether I had a disease which was wasting away my muscles and causing me to run poorly.

The first I knew about this was when I returned to the Empire Village after playing golf and found a note on my bed asking me to report to Pat Sage, the English team manager. He told me of the observations he had received from Watts. It was decided I should see the team doctor. My legs were measured and it was found there was a difference of three-quarters of an inch in width and length, between the left and the right. The doctor pointed out that this was common with soccer players who favour one foot more than the other.

Nevertheless, it was decided I should go to the Canadian Medical Research Centre, which had been set up in the Empire Village, for a complete check-up. They decided there was plenty of power in my legs—as much as most wrestlers and weight-lifters. Once again I was given a hundred-per-cent bill of health. So much for the 'withered leg'.

I consider I owe most of my success in athletics to the help I received in the R.A.F. during the two years from December 1954. After a short stay at Cardington, I went to Hednesford, Staffordshire. There, all the recruits were assembled in a camp theatre for a general talk. Afterwards all those interested in sport were asked to stay behind. The R.A.F. are fitness-mad, and I found wonderful facilities for cross-country running near Hednesford. There was a forest outside the camp which was wonderful for training.

For the first time in my life I began to train properly for running. It was not long before I was the best runner on the camp, beating Bill McMinnis, a former A.A.A. marathon champion. I owe a lot to a Scottish corporal, who encouraged my cross-country running.

After finishing my square-bashing, I stayed on at Hednesford for an extra week to compete for them in the R.A.F. Championships. While I was changing for this race, I heard a short man, in civilian clothes, remark, 'I think R.A.F. Yatesbury will win this team race.'

'You haven't seen Hednesford,' I said. 'They'll wipe up Yatesbury.'

'By the way, Ibbotson, I'm Squadron-Leader Davis,' he said.

On the advice of other Service athletes, I had written to a Squadron-Leader D. C. Davis, who I had been told was the man who could most assist my athletics career in the R.A.F.

'I think you're coming down to join me when you leave Hednesford,' he said, clearing up the confusion.

Yatesbury did win the team race, and we were second. Squadron-Leader Davis was proved right as he usually is. In the months which were to follow he proved the most important influence in my sporting life. A former Universities of Wales half-mile champion, he had a sound knowledge of all track and field events. He was an educational officer in the Service, and also an A.A.A. honorary coach.

It was Squadron-Leader Davis who introduced me to interval training, which has done so much to improve middle-distance running. This is based on covering a specified distance after a timed rest. It had helped Roger Bannister break four minutes for the mile.

Squadron-Leader Davis gave me a training schedule for cross-country running which was also aimed to help me build up for the track the following season. He was a brilliant organizer. We were given training tickets which meant that when we finished our technical work—I was on a radar course—we could go out training immediately and have a properly cooked meal later. But for these we would have had to have tea with the rest of the unit and then have to wait a couple of hours before being able to train.

Also, I was given a bunk to myself, a privilege usually reserved for N.C.O.s, so that I could put in enough sleeping hours.

Throughout my Service career I preferred to remain an aircraftman as promotion would have incurred extra duties.

The Station Commander at Yatesbury was keen on cross-country running, and I was often called to his office after a race to be congratulated. This sort of encouragement made me want to do even better.

There were many fine athletes at Yatesbury, including David Thornton, later to become the Inter-Varsity half-mile champion; Roy Darchambaud, of South London Harriers; Roy Frampton, a Surrey low-hurdler; Ian Gurney, another Blue; and Bobby Longstaff, from Darlington. Longstaff was a cook and used to help with our food.

After a successful cross-country season, which included being third in the Yorkshire, fourth at the R.A.F. Championships, and eighth in the Northern Championships, I was anxious to get on the track to see whether this scientific training programme would produce results.

You can imagine my joy when I received the following letter from Martin Walmsley, a student at Manchester University:

'We are holding a special 2,000 metres race in conjunction with the Universities Athletic Union Championships at the White City, Manchester, to help draw the crowd. As you have been running well this winter, we have decided to invite you along with Gordon Pirie and John Disley. All expenses will be paid.'

6

I make the headlines

Ibbotson proved to me the moment he took the lead he had the right spirit. His 2,000 metres' time of 5 min. 8·8 sec. also indicated he would be a champion. A short talk with this fair-haired Yorkshireman proved conclusively that he not only had the physical assets, but also the right mental approach.—*Tom Goodman, Manchester Evening Chronicle*

THE other lads in Hut Y46 at Yatesbury ribbed me about competing against such Olympic runners as Gordon Pirie and John Disley.

'You're only in as a filler, so don't get a swollen head,' one Lancashire lad joked.

That weekend I went home to Huddersfield and had to borrow £1 from my mother for the fare to Manchester. On arrival at the White City, I discovered that the invitation runners had a dressing-room of their own. I felt I must have reached the big-time. Pirie and Disley were known to me only by reputation, and they ignored me when they discussed what times to run the different laps on the small Manchester track. Maybe it was a good thing because I had no idea how to run a 2,000-metre race, and did not want to betray my ignorance. Also I doubt whether they would have considered me good enough as my best mile time at that period was 4 min. 16 sec. I had decided that the only thing to do was to hang on to second or third position, and set my mind on the task of not getting dropped.

In 1952, when I ran against Alan Parker, a finalist in the Olympic 5,000 metres in Helsinki, I managed to stay with him until the last lap. If a runner is dropped by the leaders he cannot normally get back in touch again. There is no point in trying to save a sprint finish if you are too far back to use it. It is strange that many runners allow themselves to fall back, and then do not lose ground when a hundred yards back. Psychologically it is better to stay up in front because if the leader tries to break away you are in a position to go with him.

If you are capable of running two miles in nine minutes, then there is no reason why you can't do this even in a three-mile race. Some runners get worried when they hear the interval times, and seem to think they will not be able to finish. When I broke the European mile record at Glasgow, in 1957, Mike Berisford was up with me at the half-way mark, and then he seemed to panic because the race was exceptionally fast, and I finished fifty yards ahead of him. Earlier that year I had beaten him by only a few feet, although admittedly in a slower time. However, I do not believe I was that much better than Berisford in Glasgow. All this proves that the psychology of running is just as important as the physical aspects. One must counteract the tendency of the mind to shy at the prospect of making greater demands on the body.

As arranged, John Disley led for the earlier part of the race, and then Pirie took over. I found I could keep with him comfortably, and a furlong from the mile mark I took the plunge and raced into the lead. 'Just a filler, was I?' Tactically it would have been better for me to have waited until the last 220 yards, but then I was anxious to get a good mile time, and I was thus delighted when I heard I had passed this mark in 4 min. 8·8 sec. I knew, as we neared the end of the race, Pirie would challenge, so I sprinted to make it more difficult for him. When he began his drive for the tape, I had no answer, but I was quite content to come second.

This race did me an immense amount of good, and proved I was training on the right lines. It also widened my horizon—maybe I could manage the mile in 4 min. 5 sec.

For the first time the Press became an influence in my life. It was flattering to read my name linked with Pirie's, and friends no longer had to be told about the race as they could read it for themselves. On my return to Yatesbury, I received the following letter from Air Vice-Marshal J. L. F. Fuller-Good:

'Dear Ibbotson,

1. I was delighted to read of your magnificent battle with D. A. G. Pirie in the 2,000 metres at the White City, Manchester, on Saturday, 21st May, 1955.

Cross-country running lays the foundation for fast miles. *Above:* Ibbotson leading Olympic marathon champion Alain Mimoun (France), Fred Norris (England), Marcel Van de Wattyne (Belgium) and Eddie Bannon (Scotland) in the international race at Belfast in 1956. *Below:* C. Wilson hands over to Ibbotson, his South London Harriers team-mate, in the London to Brighton relay in 1957

Ibbotson is left to do the donkey work in the match against Hungary at the White City in 1955. Tucked in behind him are Chris Chataway, Laszlo Tabori (hidden by Chataway) and Erno Beres

2. To be beaten for first place by the narrow margin of twenty yards by one of the world's greatest middle-distance runners, whose time was only 2·8 seconds slower than the present world record, is, I consider, one of the finest performances put up by any past or present R.A.F. athlete.

3. You have achieved fame for yourself and brought credit to the Royal Air Force, and I shall follow your future performances with much interest.

4. Good luck to you.

Yours sincerely,

J. L. F. Fuller-Good.'

What a great human Service is the R.A.F. I felt as proud to belong to it as if I had been an Air Vice-Marshal myself. That letter gave me tremendous encouragement for the Inter-Counties Championships, to be held at the White City, London, the following week, when I was due to represent Yorkshire in the three miles. Before this race I ran in a mid-week Service meeting over 880 yards on a bumpy track, but still attained my fastest time of 1 min. 57 sec.

Pirie did not take part in the Inter-Counties three miles, which was disappointing for I no longer regarded him as an athlete outside my sphere. Even so, there were a number of fine athletes competing, including Ken Norris and Frank Sando. They are two of the best cross-country and long-distance runners that Britain has ever produced. I was so intent upon keeping up with these two that I ran wide almost all the three miles. It was a wonderful experience when I discovered I had more speed at the end, and won my first race at London's White City. My time of 13 min. 34·6 sec. was less than three seconds slower than the British record, and only 8·2 seconds outside the world best, held by Vladimir Kuts of Russia.

Afterwards I met Franz Stampfl, the Austrian-born coach who guided Roger Bannister, Chris Brasher and Chris Chataway to fame. He told me I had the ability to become a world champion, and promised to send me some training schedules. Unfortunately, he was due to leave for Australia within a few weeks, and as I was stationed at Yatesbury, it was going to be difficult to meet. I think it is essential for an athlete to be in direct contact with a coach. So, though Stampfl helped me with training ideas, he never actually coached me.

D

In the evening I celebrated with a couple of friends, and allowed myself two sherries. I remember that my dad told me the Yorkshire runners of his day used to train on sherry and eggs.

On the Whitsun Bank Holiday Monday I ran one of the few six-mile races of my career. I was encouraged to run such a distance as it is good for building up stamina. The Hungarian, Sandor Iharos, and Gordon Pirie have shown that it is possible to achieve world-class times from 1,500 metres to 10,000 metres. But I found it was boring running for twenty-four laps. My determination not to be dropped helped, and I kept up with Peter Driver and Frank Sando. But this time I was the one left without a 'kick' over the last lap, and I came third in 28 min. 52 sec.

During the next fourteen days I had ten races over 880 yards, one mile and three miles, and won them all. In fact, I did not lose again until I represented Britain for the first time in a match with Germany, and lost to Chris Chataway when he set up a world three-mile record.

In my service with the R.A.F. I became accustomed to regular competition. Not all the races were against class opposition, but I found they broke the monotony of training, and gave me the chance to experiment with tactics. Sometimes I would run in front, and at other times hang back and practise my sprint finish.

During 1955 I actually ran fifty-five races, excluding heats, but this was not harmful as many were easy races. A young runner should plan his racing programme to suit himself, and not listen to the hundred and one theories of friends.

7

Chataway ran for himself

Ibbotson gave proof that his final speed now is a dangerous weapon as well as the strength in the body of the race. Sure enough, just about the start of the 220 yards Chataway suddenly slipped past his man, grabbed the inside position for the bend, and keeping just wide of the churned-up part of the track left Ibbotson with the hideous choice of running very wide or falling behind. Ibbotson never hesitated. He came up almost level on the outside of the bend, got his nose in front with forty yards to go, and resisted the champion's last dying efforts to pass him in the last ten yards. Both could justly be proud of their struggle and Ibbotson's judgment had been gloriously vindicated.—*Larry Montague, Manchester Guardian, writing on the A.A.A. three miles in 1956*

CHRIS CHATAWAY will always remain one of the idols of the British track. Allied to his instinctive athletic talent was a huge helping of that vital quality—guts. He was called the 'Red Fox', partly because of his flowing auburn mane and partly because of his uncanny flair for track tactics. I had many great races with Chataway, and lost more than I won.

Chataway's finest race was in 1954 when he gained that epic victory over the Russian, Vladimir Kuts, who later won two Olympic titles at the Melbourne Olympic Games. In that 5,000-metre race Chataway hung on to Kuts like a limpet, and did not lead until the last ten strides, winning in a world-record time. I was one of the television audience of 12,000,000 who watched that duel under the floodlights. As I did not have a set at home, it meant a visit to the local pub where I bought a pint of shandy to last me the evening. Even today I marvel at the psychology and bulldog spirit which blended to give Chris supremacy over the Russian master.

Little did I think that in nine months I would be like Kuts,

51

struggling in vain to get away from Chris. In 1954 I was just an unknown lad, full of ambitions. In my many races with Chataway I often thought back to the duel I had seen on television, and later found myself sympathizing with Kuts.

The first time I spoke to Chataway was at the A.A.A. championships in 1955. This had already been a good season for me, and my victory at the Whitsun Inter-Counties three miles had made me one of the favourites for the National title. The Press had forecast that it would be a two-man race—between Chataway and me.

'That was a wonderful three miles that you ran at the Inter-Counties,' Chataway said while we were warming-up.

'Thanks very much. How are you?'

'I am not sure. I have not had much time to train for the three miles.'

To a virtual novice like myself, this sounded encouraging, but I later discovered that Chataway nearly always underestimated his fitness—perhaps to fool the opposition. It also lured his rivals into becoming pace-makers.

These championships were vital to me. My earlier successes had helped to build up my confidence, but only an A.A.A. title could prove I was the best in the country. Chataway had also had a good early season, including a sub-four-minute mile. This showed he would be the faster at the finish if he were still strong. The final of the A.A.A. Championships was held on one of those rare days for England, with the temperatures well up in their eighties. A deckchair by the river would have been more pleasant than running at the White City. The heat was disturbing because I knew I would have to set the pace and try to sap Chataway's strength. I was pondering on the way he had hung on to Kuts when the gun went.

Little Pat Ranger, of the R.A.F., went off at a terrific pace, and when he reached the first mile in 4 min. 25 sec. I decided it was too fast and dropped back twelve yards, with Chataway lurking a yard behind.

Ranger began to feel the heat and pace. At the half-way stage he turned his head and gasped, 'Carry on, Derek—I'm done.' So I took over with my red shadow still behind.

It had happened just as expected. I had taken over the role of Kuts. So I adopted his tactics of breaking into short bursts of fifty yards or more. But it was no good, and only hurt me. Every time I broke into a sprint Chataway came with me. I felt completely trapped, and could think of no escape. I vowed I would train even harder, but this was no consolation in the middle of the race.

When there was only a lap left, I slowed up to save something to counter the Chataway sprint I was now beginning to dread. Going down the back-straight for the last time, I felt like a family car with Stirling Moss just behind.

I was travelling at four-minute-mile speed—fifteen miles per hour—when Chataway rushed past me. If somebody had hit me in the stomach it could not have been worse. I just had no hope of beating him, and he won by twenty yards. So Chataway had proved decisively he was master that day.

But the disappointment made me determined to find a finishing burst of my own to match Chataway's.

It also encouraged me when I learnt that Chataway had said in an interview I was one of the strongest runners he had met. The incentive to beat Chataway played an important part in my progress, and because of this I owe him a debt.

Chataway to me has always been rather an enigma. Sometimes he even appeared almost to hate the sport which had brought him so much fame. He seldom competed in the small meetings which are the nurseries for stars of the future. His appearances were mainly reserved for London's glamorous White City, spectacles watched by thousands of spectators and the far-reaching television cameras. Of course, as an amateur he is entitled to please himself, but athletics would die if all internationals restricted their appearances in the same way. At least Chataway ran more frequently than his great rival, Roger Bannister, who sometimes appeared the Greta Garbo of the track.

My critics have often said I run too much, but then it gives me enjoyment even if I lose. Also, maybe, I have been a pot-hunter.

Most runners dislike leading throughout a race, but often it is inevitable, especially over three miles. Chataway loathed being in front, and as he restricted himself mainly to major meetings where the fields were normally large, it was possible for him to hide away until the last lap when he would pounce so effectively.

These tactics brought Chataway many successes, which undoubtedly boosted Britain's prestige. However, sometimes in an international match the situation demands taking the lead. This happened when I was paired with Chataway in the three-mile race against Hungary, at the White City, London, in 1956. On the Friday evening beforehand Chataway had run the mile and was beaten by Laszlo Tabori, who was also in the three miles.

The Hungarians had another fine performer in Erno Beres. So it was vital to have a fast early pace if Britain was to have the lion's share of the major points in this close international.

Before the race Chataway and myself discussed tactics. 'I am afraid we will have to lead, otherwise they'll be too fast for us at the finish,' Chataway said. He then explained that he was not a front runner, but it did not seem to affect me. 'If you lead for the first two miles I will take over for two laps to give you a rest, when you can take over again,' he suggested.

'If that is what you think is best, it's all right with me,' I replied.

I was not happy about the position because it meant that I would have little chance of winning after leading nearly all the way. However, it seemed the best plan for Britain because Chataway was the better runner, and a victory for him would mean major team-points, even if I lost.

This time it was a typical English summer day. Rain was falling when the race started, and, to make matters worse, there was a strong wind which always affects the front runner.

After only a few laps, I was covered in mud. Chataway and the Hungarians were tucked in behind, protected to a certain extent from the wind which is the middle-distance runner's Public Enemy No. 1. It is impossible to run fast times in wind because the help in one direction can never counter the hindrance in the other.

As we churned round the track, I remember I prayed for the eighth lap, when Chataway was to take over and give me a rest. As we passed the starting-line 'No. 4' was raised to indicate there was a mile to go. As planned Chataway went into the lead, and it was a wonderful relief being away from the full force of the wind and rain.

Tucked in behind Chataway my confidence returned. Running seemed little effort now. I had covered only half a lap in this comfortable position and was confident I could nurse my energies for the final assault, when Chataway swung into an outside lane and shouted, 'You take it, Derek.'

I had no choice but to go back into the lead. And I was flaming mad. My rhythm and mental attitude towards the race changed immediately. Chataway had let me down by not sticking to the plan. I would have been much better if I had led all the way. My only consolation was that it should help Chataway to win for Britain and I might be able to hang on for third place. At that stage I had no pretensions about beating Tabori.

Instinctively I slowed up the race, and the pace was a crawl when we reached the start of the final lap. Still the other competitors ran mutely behind. With 300 yards left, I tried to sprint in a vain hope of holding off Tabori and Chataway. It was no good. They came rushing past me and fought out a thrilling duel.

The Hungarian just won with a final lap of 57 seconds, but Chataway clocked the same time of 13 min. 44·6 sec. A hundred yards from the tape I was overtaken by Beres, so the Hungarians gained seven points to four from the race, and I was last.

'Sorry I could not help, Derek, but the wind and rain were too much for me, and I wanted to conserve myself to ensure that we got a win,' said Chataway afterwards.

I'm afraid I lost a lot of respect for Chris after that match. It was not that I objected to leading to help my country, but Chataway's tactical alteration to our plan upset me, and might have prevented an individual third place. It would have been better if we had agreed for me to lead all the way. Then I would have known where I stood. A few weeks previously against Germany I had also partnered Chataway over the three miles. This was the first international of my career, and was a much happier affair. A couple of days after being selected for this match at the White City I received a letter from Chataway. It read as follows:

'Dear Derek,
      I am so glad we are to run together against the Germans. I have been thinking about it a bit though, and have a plan, about which I should be glad to have your comments.
      As you know the way in which I prefer to run my races, and the way in which I produce the best results, is to leave other people to do all the work and run behind until the last lap. But there does not seem to be much point in just doing this in this match. For one thing I don't believe that the Germans will

provide us with much opposition. Schade has been quite good, but he has gone off a lot recently, and apart from him I don't think they've got anybody.

I reckon we ought to try and get inside this world record. It is not after all a very good one, and I am sure we can both manage it. What I suggest is this—that we should lead alternate laps. I will lead the first and you the second and so on. Then in the last two laps we can race it out against each other.

I think we should aim for the first mile in around 4 min. 27 sec., getting to the two miles in about 8 min. 58 sec.—in fact, except for the first and last laps, aim at a fraction under 68 sec. for each. I find it very tiring to lead during a race and I believe that when it comes to the finish it will be a very close one between us. But I think it is an ideal opportunity to have a shot at this record; and it will be good preparation for our race against Kuts in Moscow, which may be a good deal faster.

I wonder what you think about this. If you wanted to ring me up, I shall be at work, otherwise perhaps you could drop me a line.

Whatever we decide, I think it best not to say anything to anybody. As once the Press get hold of it everything is ruined.

I hope you are well, and that you did not have any after-effects from last Saturday's heat.

With best wishes,
Yours,
Chris Chataway.'

I was delighted and honoured to be asked by such a famous colleague to attempt a world record in my first international. Immediately I sat down and wrote a proposed schedule with the following times for the twelve laps—63, 67, 68, 68, 68, 68, 68, 68, 68, 67, 65, 62. This meant the different miles would be covered in 4 min. 26 sec., 4 min. 32 sec., and 4 min. 22 sec., for a total time of 13 min. 20 sec., which was seven seconds under Kuts's world record.

So I wrote to Chataway and said I would be happy to join him in a world record attempt, and suggested the times I had outlined. He replied:

'Dear Derek,

Many thanks for your letter. I am glad you are willing to have a shot. I agree completely with your schedule except that I doubt whether we shall manage the last 880 yards in 2 min. 7 sec.

All we have to do now then is to hope for a fine day on Saturday with no wind. We can decide on the day who is going to take the odd laps and who the even—not that it makes much difference.

I see that Schade did 14 min. 18 sec. for 5,000 metres last Saturday, which is not too bad. The other lad has done about the same. But I doubt very much whether they can keep up after the first mile and a half. Schade likes leading though, and he might get off at the right pace. Still we shall see, and we can talk about it while warming up on Saturday. I'll be there at 3.30.

Yours,
Chris.'

The plan worked perfectly. Chris took the first lap in a slowish 67 seconds, but we soon made up the time and passed the mile in the suggested 4 min. 26 sec. By the eighth lap I was beginning to feel the strain and this quarter-mile took me almost 70 seconds. But when Chris took over again I had no difficulty in running the quarter in 68 seconds, which proves the value of trailing behind. It might have been better if Chris had gone on his own then because I laboured 71 seconds over the tenth lap, and was in no condition to fight for the world record, which was now within our grasp.

At this stage the two Germans were a long way back, and Chris went off like a panther for a brilliant final half-mile in 2 min. 5·4 sec. (yes, he had underestimated his own ability) and created the world record in 13 min. 23·2 sec.

Just at the time when I was going to challenge Chris, I stumbled on the kerb of the track, and after this was satisfied to finish second. I tired badly over the last half-mile, and finished more than a hundred yards behind. I even fell over near the tape. It was obvious I was not ready for such running then, but I had helped Chris to set a world and British record which I would be out to break later in my career.

Chris was very generous in his praise for the part I had played. When the British team went to Moscow for the first full international with the Soviet Union, the match was put on in one day instead of the normal two, so Kuts decided to run, and win, the 10,000 metres against Gordon Pirie. This was a disappointment to Chris and myself. We had been looking forward to meeting this fine athlete.

In this race we decided the best tactics were to let the Russians do the leading. Chris told me not to run too close to him for fear of being spiked. I found it strange running a race in a rear position, and no doubt it was my impatience to get into the lead which made me go too early. Chris overtook me, and the better of the two Russians, Ivan Chernyavskiy, followed him. I did not have enough fight left, and so was third.

This was the end of a long season for me. In the spring I had hardly been known as a runner outside Yorkshire. Now I had run four times for Britain, but I still had a tremendous amount to learn. I decided that the first priority was to find a sprint like Chataway's at the end of a race. The method of lengthening my stride was not successful because it did not give enough extra speed. What I wanted was a real 'kick'.

The Olympic Games were to be held the following year, and during the winter of 1955–6 I trained harder than ever before. I was in the R.A.F. at the time and stationed in Wiltshire, where the rolling downs were ideal for cross-country work. I enjoyed my best cross-country season but all the time I was working hard to find a sprint to beat Chataway.

My first race in 1956 was at Hampden Park during the interval of the England-Scotland soccer international, and I ran the last lap of a two-mile race in 56 seconds which proved to me that I was beginning to find the answer to my quest.

When I arrived at the A.A.A. Championships that year to meet Chataway again, I was in the right frame of mind. *Athletics Weekly* had sent me a questionnaire, and this included a request for my greatest race. I had deliberately not sent it on, because I had wanted to say, 'Beating Chataway for the first time.' Chataway was now a leading television personality, and he told me he was not very fit. It was true he had run only one race so far that season, but I was taking no chances. Never underestimate any opponent, especially somebody in Chataway's class.

Before the Championships there was a lot of speculation whether Gordon Pirie would run in the three miles. A week previously he had told me, with that deceptive smile of his, 'It would be a good race to run in because we could then both grind Chataway into the ground.' Knowing Pirie, that was his ambition.

I did not see Pirie during the warm-up before the race, so I assumed that he had scratched. It was not that I was frightened of him competing but his presence might have made me alter my tactics. These were clear in my mind. They had been worked out during the long winter runs over the Wiltshire downs. They were simply to run in front, and dictate the race to my own liking. I was not out for records, but only to beat Chataway, and put myself into line for Olympic selection.

For the first half-mile Mike Maynard and Mike Schofield led. Then I took over. Of course Chataway was there on my shoulder. This time I was happy he was with me. What is more I wanted him to be as good as he was on the night he beat Kuts. Chataway was the greatest fighter on the track, and I wanted to conquer him at his best.

It must be difficult for someone who has never taken part in a major track race to understand the feelings of competitors. A boxer would be conscious of the loneliness which sometimes isolates the athlete from the thousands of people in the stadium. The only beings he is aware of are the other runners—the enemy.

There is no room for the Corinthian spirit that 'it is just a game'. Winning *is* important. And to reach the top all one's resources of courage, determination and even passion must be harnessed to achieve their greatest impact. Chataway, the man I was planning to beat in the 1956 A.A.A. Championships, had proved many times he could draw on these hidden qualities to an almost superhuman degree. That is what made this race so exciting.

As lap followed lap the thrill inside me reached an even higher pitch. Instead of dreading the finish and Chataway's final onslaught, I was impatient for it to arrive. I savoured the knowledge that now I, too, had the power to make a devastating finish. Like a child who has received his first bicycle and is hoping to display it to his friends.

I had kept the pace even because I felt it would give me a better chance. That is the only consolation for the leader—he decides the tempo. Normally I slow down just before the bell to prepare for the final lap. This time I kept the pressure on. I was determined not to give Chataway a rest. As we swept past the clanging bell, I could see a blur of faces. At this stage of the race it is impossible to hear anything, but the open mouths told me a great cheer was going up.

Rain had been falling most of the meeting, but I would have been unaware of an earthquake. The only thing that mattered was beating Chataway. As we entered the back-straight (just over 300 yards left) I remember thinking I must keep my head. I was convinced Chataway would try his famous sprint from the point where the 220-yard races now start at the White City. When we reached this spot, I moved with him and he had a surprised expression on his face as I turned right and found him on the outside lane. We were both travelling at the same speed.

Entering the final bend, I was shocked to find I was confronted with running over a part of the track which was covered in depressions filled with water. This had been all right during the normal tempo of the three-mile running but now I was on my toes sprinting. So I decided to let Chataway pass, thinking he would claim the inside berth, not knowing of its precarious footing. But Chataway was too wily. He went in front but stayed in the second lane. So I was forced out even wider for my final effort to win.

It was like holding on to a runaway horse. Entering the final straight (about 60 yards left) I was still about two feet behind. He was giving me a hell of a fight. With the tape in view I made an all-out burst and inch by inch managed to get my chest in front. But Chataway was still not finished. He fought back and we were level with only twenty yards to go. Brian Shenton, the former sprinter, had told me always to relax in a desperate finish. It is like trying to smile when someone is twisting your arm. But I did manage a grin to avoid my neck muscles tightening up. And I was able to keep my grin because I made it with a foot to spare. We both clocked the same time of 13 min. 32·6 sec.

I was a British champion at last!

8

My first four-minute mile

And suddenly, by a trick of eyesight, the other eleven
runners seemed to dissolve like insubstantial wraiths and
there was only the flying figure in the pale-blue vest . . .
coming into the straight lane of the hundred-yard course,
he had something like fifteen seconds to spare and he was
going to do it . . . he was going to . . . going to . . . BY GLORY
HE'D DONE IT!—*Peter Wilson, Daily Mirror, describing
Ibbotson's first four-minute mile*

ALTHOUGH I was A.A.A. Champion for the three miles, I
was not originally chosen for Britain in this event against
Czechoslovakia at the White City in 1956. The selectors
named Chris Chataway and Gordon Pirie. Jack Crump, the British
team manager, wrote me a personal letter and explained that the
Board felt that it was important that Chataway should have every
chance of running against international opposition before the
Olympic Games because his work had prevented him taking part
in many competitions during the season.

Here is an extract from the letter:

'It is not normal and I would, in the majority of cases, have
great objections to the selectors giving any athlete the reasons
for his selection or non-selection, but, in your case, I felt it
would be right if I told you the circumstances underlying your
non-selection *at this stage* for Great Britain *v.* Czechoslovakia.
May I say, right from the outset, that we are all delighted and
well satisfied with your form, and we have no doubts whatsoever
as to your merit and ability to represent your country with
distinction in any three-mile or 5,000-metre race. But the
circumstances surrounding the Czechoslovakian match are that

we can enter only two in this event, and we have felt that we should give an opportunity to Gordon Pirie to show himself fit and able because of the other international matches and because of Olympic selection. We have taken into consideration the amount of racing which you have been doing, and we are satisfied that you have done sufficient, and that an over-surfeit of running, particularly at three miles and 5,000 metres at this stage of the season, might not be in your best interests. We are also anxious to give Chris Chataway another run at the three miles distance, for you will appreciate that, good as his performance was in running so close to you, he has not had the competition which he requires and it may be a little difficult for him, because of his B.B.C. commitments, to get competition later in August when we hope we can give it to you.

Now I am mentioning all this because I do not want you to think for one moment that you have been dropped or passed over. The contrary is, in fact, the case, and I hope that you will stand by just in case we find that Gordon Pirie is not fit enough to run, in that instance we should, of course, have no hesitation in putting you in the three miles. But another reason why we have decided not to put you in the three miles is because we are anxious to give you a one-mile race on the Monday in the "Emsley Carr Mile" and you will be receiving an invitation to run in this race.'

Naturally he did not mention, unlike some sections of the Press, that it would give the British public a chance to see one of the rare races between Chataway and Pirie. I had already met Chataway that year, and therefore another clash might not have had the same box-office value. It is hard for an athlete to appreciate these views, and I don't see why he should. I wanted every opportunity to run in top-class competition as the Olympic Games were just as important to me as to Chataway and Pirie.

To stay in the top class as an amateur, sacrifices have to be made by the individual. If Chataway was fully occupied with his career, that was his business. At the same time it did not seem right that I should suffer. I was at the start of my international athletic career and it meant everything to me.

This is typical of the many instances which cause friction between officials and athletes. The best man on form should always be selected. However, if there are special circumstances, they should be announced publicly, otherwise people might think an athlete has been dropped for some reason apart from performances. As it was, Crump asked me not to disclose to the Press the reason for my omission. I believe it is always better if the full facts are disclosed, then controversies might be avoided.

I remember a friend asking me whether I was going on holiday in August, and I asked, 'What gave you that idea?'

'Well, you're not in the British team, so I thought you must be going away,' he said.

'I wasn't selected.'

'But you're the A.A.A. champion, you *must* be nominated.' He paused for a moment. A glint came into his eye, and he added: 'What have you been up to? Had a row with one of the selectors, I suppose.'

I told him about Chataway and the letter which Crump had sent, but I knew he did not believe me.

In the end I did run as neither Chataway nor Pirie was available. I was paired with Ken Norris, who had an excellent record and always excelled in top races.

Before the meeting I had another upset—my first big row with Madeleine. To complicate everything, I was staying with Madeleine's folks in Feltham. Madeleine was also competing at the White City, and the row upset both of us. On the Saturday morning we travelled together to the stadium, but did not speak. And when Madeleine decides to shut up, an oyster isn't in it.

Many runners rely a lot on nervous energy, but normally I never get keyed up. This time it was different. I was all on edge for the start of the three miles, so that I could forget my domestic worries.

Ken Norris and I agreed that it would aid our chances of Olympic selection if we could break 13 min. 30 sec., and we planned to share the lead. The great Emil Zatopek was not in the Czech team, as he was still recovering from a hernia operation, and our two rivals were Mirko Graf and Milo Tomis.

If Zatopek had been running, I doubt if he would have allowed Ken and myself to dictate the race as we did. The two Czechs were happy to permit us to make the pace, and by the half-way stage only Graf was left. He remained in third position while Ken and I kept switching the lead to ensure we kept to the schedule we had set.

Approaching the final lap, Ken was in the lead and I was at his shoulder. This meant Graf would have to run wide to overtake. At least that is what we thought. But he had other ideas. He swept inside, and as I felt him come through, I shouted, 'Watch out, Ken, he's coming on the inside.'

It was too late. Ken reacted slowly, and the Czech caught his elbow. The crowd booed, but Ken was partly to blame for leaving such a wide gap. Even so, the incident annoyed me, and whipped me into an even more nervous state. I answered the call of the screaming spectators by sprinting after Graf.

There was a temptation to go straight into the lead, although still on the bend, but experience held sway and I waited until the start of the back-straight. With 300 yards left I reached Graf's shoulder. He showed no resistance and I was away. Just before taking the final bend, I turned and saw Graf was way back in second position, with Norris third.

My winning time in that race was the best I had ever recorded— 13 min. 28·2 sec.—but I still felt a little disappointed as I was a long way, five seconds, off Chataway's British record, which I had helped him to set up in the match against Germany in 1955. However, I had the consolation of knowing that my time was the second fastest ever by a British runner, and better than Gordon Pirie's best. This augured well for the Olympic Games.

When I went to get my award, Ron Bacchus, one of the organizers of the meeting on behalf of the *News of the World*, asked me whether I was competing in the Emsley Carr Mile on the Bank Holiday Monday. I had accepted an invitation to run in this event before being nominated for the three miles. But I did not think it wise to run on Monday, and told Bacchus: 'I would like to watch instead, it should be a pleasant change. Anyway, I am not really a miler.'

'Then you have a chance to prove you are,' he said.

I then remembered Madeleine's cousin, Maureen, was visiting England from Boston, U.S.A., and she wanted to go to the banquet after the meeting. 'Is there any likelihood of getting an extra ticket for the banquet?' I asked Bacchus.

With a wry smile, he said, 'If you run in the mile, I think we might be able to manage that little request.'

Chataway pipped. Ibbotson gives his all to seize victory in the three miles at the
A.A.A. Championships in 1956

First time through the four-minute barrier. Ibbotson waits at Ian Boyd's shoulder to pounce to a surprise victory in the Emsley Carr mile at the White City in 1956. His time was 3 min. 59·4 sec., equalling Roger Bannister's record

'That's bribery and corruption, but I'll think it over,' I joked.

During the week-end Madeleine and I made our peace. We spent Sunday at Kingston, Surrey, at the home of an aunt of mine, and discussed whether I should run the mile. I told her about the conversation I had had with Ron Bacchus, and we agreed that I might just as well compete to ensure that Maureen could go to the banquet. Like most Americans, she wanted to 'do the lot' while in England.

In the dressing-room before the mile, many of the competitors grouped in a huddle, working out a plan to run a fast pace to help Ian Boyd gain a place in the Olympic Games team. Outside this group, changing by himself, was the favourite, Ron Delany, a young Irishman who was studying in the United States. Earlier that year he had run the mile in 3 min. 59 sec. Since returning home he had been injured, but such an outstanding athlete could not be under-estimated.

The 'plotters' agreed that Peter Clark, a natural front runner at the time, should lead over the first lap. Then John Disley, already certain of a place at Melbourne, as a steeplechaser, would take over until the half-mile mark. Alan Gordon, a young Oxford University athlete, was prepared to help his Dark Blue colleague, Boyd, over the critical third lap which is always the toughest in any mile race. Gordon had experience of this as one of the pace-makers in the 1955 triple-four-minute mile, when Laszlo Tabori, Chris Chataway and Brian Hewson broke the 'barrier'.

Nobody bothered to consult me. Maybe they did not think I was good enough. My best time for a mile at that stage was only 4 min. 7 sec., and I was considered more a distance runner. However, this did not prevent me from thinking I could win. One must always believe in one's power to conquer.

In the early stages everything went as planned in the dressing-room. Clark towed the field round the first lap in 59·2 seconds, and Disley was in the front at the half-mile, passed in 2 min. 0·2 sec. Then Gordon led the battle with the clock. All the time I stayed up with the leaders. When Gordon was in front I thought the pace was not fast enough, and told him to get a move on. It had dawned on me I had a good chance of a fast time myself, and I was excited. Again I asked Gordon to go faster, but he gasped, 'I'm on my knees.' A hundred yards later Boyd made his bid, and I followed.

E

Victory now seemed in my grasp, but I was worried about Delany. In any race where there is a class-runner competing, you are always 'aware' of his presence. I tried to tell myself to forget Delany, and get on with the race. I couldn't, and fear that he would soon be at my shoulder drove me past Boyd before we reached the bell. I did not realize that the Irishman was in trouble and running badly.

Once in the lead, my thoughts were jumbled with figures. I remembered that we had passed the half-way stage in around two minutes, and therefore a fast time seemed almost certain. But how fast? As I moved into the final lap, the crowd's cheers swept over me like a warm current of air. Spectators can help an athlete in the same way as an audience can inspire actors. My one fear now was a late challenge, and this drove me even faster. Nearing the final bend, a chap who looked like Raymond Glendenning, but later turned out to be Leslie Edwards, a well-known athletics official, shouted to me, 'You can break four minutes—get a move on!'

This was the first time I had ever thought about this magic barrier. But I still had other problems. Where was Delany? He was the only competitor in the race who had broken four minutes, and so it was inevitable that I should believe that he would be at my shoulder. He was also famous for his finish, and later that year was to win the Olympic 1,500-metre title with a tremendous final sprint. The last hundred yards of any race are always exciting when you are in the lead. You drain everything from your body in a final assault, and thoughts disappear in a blurred agony of effort and pain.

As I burst through the tape, Jack Crump dashed up, embraced me and said: 'You've done it. You've broken four minutes! You should be all right for Melbourne now!'

But I saw only Madeleine. She was still on the track after helping to create a new British 3 × 880 yards relay record. We embraced and kissed. It was a happy moment for both of us, and a wonderful ending to what had had the makings of a disastrous week-end.

The time was announced as 3 min. 59·4 sec.—equalling Roger Bannister's English record, established when he first broke the four-minute mile. I did not feel exhausted, and knew then I could run faster. I might have done so in this race, had I known of my own ability and not worried so much about Delany. All kinds of thoughts were racing through my mind as I pulled on my track-suit. There was now a chance I might be chosen for the 1,500 and 5,000 metres in Melbourne. At the time the British All-Comers mile record was held by the Hungarian, Tabori, in 3 min. 59 sec., and I was now determined to beat this. Like most other athletes, I had always wanted to be successful over the classical mile, but had never considered myself good enough. Now, without any specialized training, I had broken four minutes. Roger Bannister kindly wrote me the following letter:

'Dear Derek,
            I had hoped to see you yesterday to congratulate you after your magnificent mile race, but unfortunately could not find you afterwards. I just want to let you know how thrilled I was that you should be the fourth Englishman to break the four minutes, and be the first to equal my record—which I am sure will not last long. My wife has promised to design a tie which shall be the membership badge of the Four-Minute Mile Club.

I hope that you will rest on your laurels now until the Olympic Games. No other races matter to you now, and with the tremendous racing season you have had I am sure you will feel like easing off a little before the final preparations for Melbourne.

Again many congratulations, and best wishes for the future.
                                        Yours sincerely,
                                        Roger Bannister.'

I did not share the same views on running as Roger, and for me a new avenue of athletics had opened up now I was Britain's fastest current miler. The mile had always been the star event of meetings in Britain so I could now expect better invitations. There are many advantages in running the mile as compared to the three miles. It takes less out of the runner and so one can compete more often. Roger had prepared himself in a different way, and believed an athlete could only produce a maximum of three top-class performances a season.

The three miles has not the same glamour, but it demands shrewder tactics than the mile, where you can stay in the third or fourth place until the last six hundred yards when you move into a position for the final strike. The approach to the three miles is much more varied. You can either go straight into the lead, following the example of such masters as Emil Zatopek or Vladimir Kuts and put in fresh bursts of sprinting when anyone stays with you, or, alternatively, you can run behind the leader and dictate the race, keeping near to his shoulder. This always gives you a psychological advantage because your opponent considers you are the fresher; he cannot see you and often feels like a fly caught in a web.

The mile lacks all this, and therefore is not so interesting for the runner. I am convinced you must know more about running to compete successfully over the longer race. All the pretentious theories on mile tactics were exploded in 1958 with the advent of Herb Elliott. He reduced miling to its simplest form—the fastest man wins. In major events like the European or Olympic Games there is nearly always somebody prepared to make the pace, and the best man on the day wins.

Ken Wood, in my view, was the forerunner of Herb Elliott. His tactics in the mile were to go away just before the end of the first lap. If he had been more tenacious and had started earlier, I think he would have been more successful.

Another point about tactics is that they are never so important to the favourite because he has something in reserve. During Elliott's fabulous season in 1958 when he set new world records for the mile and 1,500 metres, and broke four minutes no less than ten times, he looked unbeatable. In fact, he *could* be beaten over the four-lap race. If athletics ever produced the invincible man, it would lose its interest. Likewise, I have never entered a race, even during spells of my worst form, feeling I would lose. When I reach that stage I will retire.[1]

---

[1] Ibbotson was the ninth man in the world to break four minutes. He followed Roger Bannister, John Landy, Laszlo Tabori, Chris Chataway, Brian Hewson, Jim Bailey (Australia), Ron Delany, Gunnar Nielsen (Denmark). What a tribute to British athletics that it should produce four of the first nine in this achievement. And Landy, Bailey and Delany are of the same English-speaking family.

9

Selected for Melbourne

In an era which has produced so many middle-distance men
Ibbotson is undoubtedly the most natural athlete of the lot,
and one who shows least distress after a punishing performance.—*Cliff Webb, writing in the Daily Herald*

'IT LOOKS like the Queen is inviting you to take tea at Buckingham
Palace,' said an R.A.F. sergeant when he handed me a letter
with the Royal crest on the envelope.

The invitation was not to tea, but it told me I had been selected
to run for Britain at the Melbourne Olympic Games in 1956, and
was signed Philip, Duke of Edinburgh. This was one letter I
yearned to receive, and the fact that it was signed by the Duke of
Edinburgh made it even more wonderful. I am not an autograph
hunter, but this is one signature which will always be treasured.
The only other autographs I have kept are those of Sir Laurence
Olivier (we met going to Glasgow a few years ago), Ella Fitzgerald,
a singer I admire, and the jazz pianist Oscar Peterson.

In my time I have signed thousands of autographs. I seldom
refuse, but it takes an immense amount of time, and often prevents
athletes from warming-down after a race, a process which is just as
important as limbering-up beforehand. Ken Norris, the Olympic
10,000-metre runner, collected a lot of money for the fund to send
British athletes to Melbourne by charging sixpence for every autograph.

The day I received the Duke of Edinburgh's letter I went out
training, as if the Olympics were to be held the following week
instead of being almost three months away. Much has been written
about the Olympic Games being too commercial for a festival of
amateur sport. When I heard of my selection I would have given

69

every penny I possessed not to lose the opportunity to run, and if need be I would have worked my own passage to Melbourne. To an athlete the Olympic Games will always be the summit.

My only worry was whether I should be better in the 1,500 metres rather than the 5,000 metres. Before running my first four-minute mile, I had always thought I was more suited for the longer distance, but now I was not sure. Of course, I would have preferred to run in both events, but this would have meant Ian Boyd losing a place in the 1,500 metres, as at that time each nation could only enter three men for each event. Ken Wood and Brian Hewson were Britain's other choices for the 1,500 metres, and there was no disputing their right to a place. There was another consideration— the 5,000 metres, which included heats, took place before the shorter event and, therefore, I could not be at my best if I ran in both.

My colleagues in the 5,000 metres were Chris Chataway and Gordon Pirie—two men who had spurred me on by their own brilliant running. Earlier in this book I have tried to trace the different races which have helped me reach athletic prominence, and the names of Pirie and Chataway often occur. Both were splendid runners, and it would be difficult enough beating either of them, but with all the world's greatest 5,000-metre competitors also lining up, I knew I was in for the race of a lifetime at Melbourne.

Before I left for Australia I was to meet Chataway twice. The first time was in September 1956 at a meeting arranged by the Mancastrian Club at the White City, Manchester. This club has played a large part in bringing top-class athletic competition to the North. Athletic enthusiasts in the South seldom realize how much more difficult it is for the Northerners to succeed when they lack the incentive of major competitions. This Manchester race was over the mile, and this was the first time I had met Chataway at the distance. Although I stumbled at the final bend, this was no excuse for not winning. It was a slow race, and I finished second, three-fifths of a second behind Chataway's winning time of 4 min. 9·2 sec.

My most important preliminary race before Melbourne was at Budapest during the Hungary-Britain international at the beginning of October. This was my second visit to Budapest, and I noticed a great difference in the city. On my previous visit the people had been restrained, and even in discussing sport would do so in a guarded fashion. Now, many restrictions had vanished and Budapest appeared to be returning slowly to the gay days it had known before the war. Politics was no longer a forbidden subject, and the Hungarians talked about the New Future now that Stalin was dead. Even their footballers admitted that they were really professionals, and were not going to defend the Olympic title they had won in Helsinki in 1952.

When I left Hungary I was thinking it was the country in which to spend a holiday. Twenty-one days later Hungary was engulfed by a revolution, and many of the men I had spoken to were killed by Russian tanks and bullets.

Hungary's mighty athletic team was also destroyed during the uprising, for many of the men who represented them at Melbourne never returned home, while others must have lost their desire for sport after the democratic aspirations of their people had been strangled.

Like most Continental countries, Hungary possesses magnificent sporting stadia which are designed to present athletics to a vast audience. The spectator can watch all the field events perfectly, and this gives tremendous encouragement to the competitor.

One of the reasons why the standard of field events is so low in Britain is lack of presentation. This is not the fault of officials because many of them have tried hard to overcome the difficulty. The real truth is that Britain has not a stadium worthy of putting on an international meeting in the correct manner. The White City, London, is the best, but it falls a long way short of the Continental standards. This stadium caters primarily for greyhound racing, with athletics as a subsidiary interest. Many foreign competitors are appalled to find there are no warming-up facilities at the White City. But, to be fair, in all my travels I have come across few stadia where so many spectators can be protected from rain.

When the British team competed in the gigantic Dynamo, in Moscow, I was amazed to find no under-cover accommodation.

'What happens when it rains?' I asked a Russian coach.

'It never does when we hold an athletics meeting,' he said. 'We pick dates when there will be no rain.'

He was right about the time when the Russia-Britain match took place, but in 1958 when the U.S.A. team competed in Moscow, a downpour on the second day of the match almost ruined the competition, and kept spectators down to a few thousand.

What is needed in Britain is a national sports stadium. This would be possible if the different sports combined. As it is, Britain has hundreds of stadia dotted around the country, but all are normally equipped for only one sport. In contrast, Continental cities go in for more sporting clubs where a number of activities take place. This means that one week there might be a soccer match, followed by a rugby game, and then an athletics meeting.

I have wandered a little from the match with Hungary. Two of our best runners, Gordon Pirie and Ken Wood, were absent. They had already been allowed to travel to Melbourne, although their presence in Budapest might have made the difference between defeat and victory.

The early departure of these two runners illustrates once again the strange inconsistencies of the British Amateur Athletic Board. Sometimes this body tends to be too hard on athletes by insisting on a team manager, even if only one man is competing abroad. When Jim Peters, at the height of his athletic fame, was invited to run in the famous Boston Marathon, a group of English people in the U.S.A. raised money for his fare. Then they discovered it was insufficient because the Board insisted upon sending a team manager. Somehow they managed to collect more money, but it seemed a little unfair on such loyal people. On other occasions, the Board, without consulting the athlete, turns down foreign invitations.

Yet on the eve of an important international, Pirie and Wood were allowed to leave for Melbourne. This was, in my view, a foolish decision in the case of Pirie, because he had not competed over 10,000 metres during the 1956 season, although this was one of his events at Melbourne.

When the Russian match in London was cancelled earlier owing to 'Nina and the Five Hats', Pirie missed his chance of running against Vladimir Kuts. I will always contend that he would have had a better chance against Kuts in the Olympic 10,000 metres, if he had run over this distance against Hungary in Budapest.

As it was Ken Norris won this event. This was some consolation because our milers were badly beaten on the first day. Brian Hewson was trapped into leading, and was then trailed all the way by Istvan Roszavolgi and Laszlo Tabori, with Ian Boyd always in fourth place. After being the pace-maker throughout, Hewson could not resist the challenge of the two Hungarians over the last hundred yards.

I was still thinking about this race the next day when I was warming-up for the 5,000 metres with Chris Chataway as my partner. It was also inevitable I should remember the last match against Hungary a year ago when Chataway had upset me, and allowed me to lead nearly all the way. This time I had decided that whatever happened I would not make the pace. Chataway seemed nervous, and even asked me how long he should take to warm-up. He was anxious about how the Hungarians would decide to run the race. They were to be represented by Sandor Iharos, one of the most brilliant runners against the watch of all time, and Miklos Szabo, a tremendous track fighter who had been rather overshadowed by Iharos, Roszavolgi and Tabori.

Iharos was the man to watch. He had held world records from 1,500 to 10,000 metres. Earlier that year he had lost his 5,000-metre world record to Gordon Pirie. What could be better than to win it back against the British? It was strongly rumoured before the meeting that Mighali Igloi, the coaching brain behind the Hungarian middle-distance runners, had set Iharos the world record as his target in this match.

I avoided discussing tactics with Chataway so that I did not have to tell him bluntly that this was the time when I would play the waiting game. Just before the start team manager Jack Crump told Chataway and myself that he expected us to get maximum points. It sounded a little ironical, because he was Secretary of the Board which had given permission for Pirie and Wood to travel early to Melbourne.

All Chataway's fears were dispelled as soon as the gun set the four-man field off on the twelve-and-a-half lap race over the orange track. Iharos showed his hand immediately. He was after that world record. This Hungarian is a delightful runner to watch. He has the straight back of a guardsman and a perfectly relaxed leg-action. Chataway fell in behind, and I followed. On the Continent lap times are given every thousand metres. Although I could not understand them, my body told me what a cracking pace was being set.

I could feel the tension among the spectators, and noticed the smile on Igloi's face as we passed him on each lap. Everything about the race pleased me. I knew this was the sort of pace which would be set in the Olympic Games, and so it was the opportunity to prove myself in advance. The other Hungarian, Szabo, was soon dropped, but at the half-way mark Chataway and I were still with Iharos.

It was like being pitted against a machine so effortlessly did the Hungarian circuit the track. But now Igloi's smile turned to a frown. The 3,000-metre mark was passed in 8 min. 12 sec.—well inside the world schedule, but the machine blew up. Soon after passing the 3,000-metre mark, Iharos slowed down to almost a trot, taking 84 seconds for the next lap. He had gambled and failed because Chataway and myself had stuck with him. The crowd knew immediately what had happened, and in their frustration at not seeing a world record, became agitated by what had now become a trotting race. Normally I would have broken into the lead soon after Iharos had cracked, but I was determined not to go in front too soon. Eventually it became even too much for Chataway, and he took over from Iharos. And then I followed. There could be no new record now, but victory would be sweet just the same. It was strange running behind Chataway. This was the first time I had observed him from behind, and I thought what an immaculate character he cut. Even when he runs his red hair remains unruffled.

Iharos remained with us, and was still an obvious danger. Chataway kept the pace down, and was no doubt thinking I would take over the lead, but I had made up my mind to wait until the last 300 metres. This I did and shot past Chataway, winning the inside berth for the final bends. I did not know at the time, but Iharos failed to respond. Chataway, however, accepted the challenge like the fighter he is, and down the final straight overtook me, and I could not pull him back. There were only a few yards in it at the tape, but Chataway had proved himself master again. I had the consolation of running one of my fastest 5,000 metres so far, of 14 minutes, and also beating Iharos who had been considered one of the favourites for the Olympic title.

Incidentally Britain lost this international by 10 points, but at least Chataway and I had provided Jack Crump with a maximum from the 5,000 metres.

After Budapest I had three more races over the 1,500 metres to sharpen up my speed for Melbourne. One of these included a victory over Tabori and Iharos during the London-Budapest match.

A number of leading British athletes were making arrangements to travel early to Australia, so as to become properly acclimatized. I asked the R.A.F. for extra leave, and it was readily granted. I will always be grateful to the Service for their helpful attitude at all times.

In the meantime I discovered that, apart from Pirie and Wood, who had already left, Chataway, Chris Brasher, Derek Johnson, Frank Sando and Thelma Hopkins were all booked to fly out early. When I wrote to Jack Crump for permission to leave, I thought it was only a formality.

It was a bitter blow when I heard from Crump that all the places in the aircraft had gone. I felt like the Odd Man Out. It was not as if I were asking for any extra financial privileges, because I was prepared to pay my own expenses in Australia until the main party arrived.

No wonder there is so much dissatisfaction in athletics. I know that a number of other Olympic athletes were hurt by the arrangements which allowed a few to travel early. Of course there were some who could not get the extra time off, but there were many others like myself who were prepared to pay their own expenses. Those who went out to Melbourne before the main party were the most successful.

Brasher won a gold medal in the steeplechase; Pirie was second in the 5,000 metres; Derek Johnson ran a magnificent race to finish with a silver medal in the 800 metres; while Thelma Hopkins was runner-up in the high jump.

In fact, I was the only individual member of the British team who went with the main party, to win a medal. The only other exceptions were the men's 4 × 400 metres relay team who were third, and the girls' sprint quartette who were runners-up to Australia.

10

Almost arrested in Athens

*In buying houses and taking a wife, shut your eyes and
commend yourself to God.*—*Italian proverb*

I SHUT my eyes and commended myself to the Almighty just
before leaving for the Melbourne Olympic Games. Taking a
similar risk was Madeleine Wooller, one of the few women in
the world who had broken five minutes for the mile.

Madeleine and I had met when we were both members of the
British team in Moscow in 1955. Our courtship was not entirely
unchequered, but surviving the usual sudden squalls was that
essential understanding of each other's differences. We both knew
the demands that athletics must make on each other's time,
and this mutual sympathy laid the foundations of our happy
marriage.

Unfortunately, there was no chance of Madeleine being selected
for the Olympic Games as her events, the 800 metres and the mile,
are not included in the programme. Women—at the time I write—
are not allowed to run over distances of more than 200 metres at
the Games, though they can swim up to 400 metres.

We decided to marry before I departed. I was due to leave on
Thursday, November 11th, and the wedding took place on the
previous Saturday. Madeleine is a Roman Catholic. She has an
Irish mother—perhaps that is where the temper comes from!—and
her father is a Londoner. When we went to see Father J. O'Brien,
the priest at St. Lawrence's Church, Feltham Green, Middlesex,
where Madeleine lived, I was struck by his resemblance to Roger
Bannister. I told him I was a Methodist, and did not wish to change
my religion. Ron Shillito, a friend of mine from Huddersfield, was
best man.

Madeleine herself had spent hundreds of hours training so she fully realized what she was letting herself in for by marrying an athlete.

We had both been proud when the French newspaper *L'Equipe* published a table based on the performances of married couples —and made us the leading pair. They used the best times the husband and wife had recorded, and then related them to the international points tables which are used for the ten-event decathlon. Madeleine and I came ahead of such brilliant combinations as the Zatopeks (Emil and Dana) and Connollys (Harold and Olga), all of whom had won individual Olympic titles.

There are many famous British athletics couples, such as John and Sylvia Disley, Geoff and Pam Elliott, Alan and Phyllis Perkins, Peter and Suzanne Allday.

Women athletes are often even more fanatical than the men. Soon after our daughter Christine was born, Madeleine was back running again. She is a great believer in weight training, and even started her own school at Huddersfield, giving youngsters the benefit of her experience.

Madeleine and I have often trained together, but it is not a good thing to do so regularly. A man must undergo more stamina- and speed-exercises than a woman. There is always the tendency for him not to train hard enough, and for the woman too much.

The journey to Melbourne was eventful as it took place during the height of the Suez crisis. Aircraft could not land at Cairo, and many diversions were necessary. Our first stop was at Athens where we remained only ninety minutes to refuel and have breakfast. But my Olympic ambitions almost ended there.

At the airport there were a number of anti-British leaflets, detailing alleged atrocities in Cyprus. Some of the water-polo players ripped up about a hundred of these. Being curious I picked up some of the fragments, and was trying to piece them together when a plain-clothes Greek official approached me.

'You have no right to tear these up,' he said in English. 'Come with me to the Airport Commander.'

He then went to take my arm, but I moved away and replied, 'No, thank you.'

John Disley was standing nearby, and joined in, 'He is not going anywhere.'

'Right then, I will call the police and have you both arrested.'

The situation looked critical, but fortunately team manager Jack Crump arrived on the spot. He turned to the Greek and said, 'If you leave leaflets like that around your international airports, they deserve to be torn up.' Then he said, 'Come on, Derek, you had better get on board the aircraft.'

The Greek was furious, and went to get the police, while I hurried to the aeroplane. Soon Greek officials were on the tarmac, demanding, 'We want that man off, otherwise we will refuse permission for this aircraft to leave.'

While I had visions of digging roads as a prisoner, instead of running at Melbourne, Crump handled the situation most competently. Somehow he calmed down the Greek officials, and I was able to continue with the team to Basra and then Karachi.

Our stay in Karachi was lengthened due to engine trouble. So most of the lads, feeling stiff from so much travelling and sitting down, decided to have a run, although it was one o'clock in the morning. All our training kit was stored away, so we stripped down to our underpants and vests. It must have been quite a sight!

An enjoyable part of the trip was the overnight stop at Singapore. We stayed at an hotel on the sea-front, and had a wonderful meal. Some of the party went for a swim, and during the evening there was dancing on the shore. We were all ordered to bed at 10 p.m. I did not need any coaxing as I was feeling the effect of malaria tablets.

By the time we reached Darwin everyone was tired. Only those who have experienced a four-day flight across the world can understand the feeling. Taking breakfast at what should be supper-time, and this combined with lack of sleep and exercise, gives one a queasy, 'upside-down' feeling.

On our arrival in Australia I met the Hungarian athletics team, who had just escaped the revolution. Naturally, they were all dejected, but covered it up by laughing and joking. The Hungarians had a wonderful record in the Olympic Games, and in 1952 won sixteen gold medals, an amazing performance for such a small country. Now they were a team full of fears. How could they prepare during the final days before the Games, when they were haunted by the horrors taking place in their country?

After meeting the Hungarians, I became confused myself. It

was ironical that the youth of the world was travelling to Melbourne to further the cause of international friendship when in some cases brothers were killing each other. During the first Olympic Games in Ancient Greece a month of peace used to be proclaimed. How wonderful if this had happened at the time of the Melbourne Olympiad!

Countries like Holland and Switzerland and Spain withdrew from the Games because of the international situation, while many competitors, even of nationalities not concerned in the world disputes, were unsettled. I am certain this atmosphere affected many performances in the days which followed.

The Hungarians decided to ignore the Russians, and the only serious trouble was when the two teams met at water-polo. Fighting broke out during the game, and the police had to intervene. This avoided a riot. It says much for the spirit of the Games that this was the only incident.

Many people doubted whether the Australians would be able to stage such a mammoth spectacle, yet they proved what a young virile nation can achieve. Naturally, everything did not run smoothly —many of the times were clocked wrongly in the 10,000 metres— but then it never does during major sporting meetings.

The accommodation at the Olympic Village, about nine miles outside Melbourne, was excellent, but there were not enough social amenities. I worked it out that if I stayed for six months, I might get one game of table-tennis. And the country which then held the Davis Cup could not provide any tennis-courts.

There were grave doubts whether all the preparations would be finished in time. In fact, when the main British team arrived, the training track at the Stadium had not been completed, and rain had turned the new grass into a swamp.

If you imagine thousands of men preparing for a world heavyweight boxing championship, then you will have some idea of the tension before an Olympiad. Everyone seemed to have worries, and the Village was alive with stories about how well someone else did in training. There was a craving to get away from it all. Unfortunately, this was not easy because Melbourne was some distance away, and the British team, unlike many others, were not provided with pocket money. This is understandable in a way as the financial burden of sending British competitors has always been borne by private subscription. Even so, it needed a protest from the British team before we managed even to have our laundry paid for, and the cost of three postcards home a week provided.

Most evenings the competitors relaxed in the main hall where concerts and dances were held. I mixed a lot with the American athletes, and indirectly received invitations from six United States universities—Stamford, Southern California, Idaho, Villanova, Houston and University College, Los Angeles. There is a lot of criticism in Europe of U.S.A. athletics scholarships, but I think they can be of immense help to a young man interested in a career and sporting success. A Yorkshire friend of mine, Reg Darley, was studying at Houston, Texas. He had emigrated to Canada, and as a comparatively good miler was able to attend a university—an opportunity which he would not get in England.

He told the Houston authorities I might be interested, and I would have gone to the United States but for my marriage—though I doubt whether I would have stayed there because of my love of England, especially Yorkshire.

American success in the Olympics can be traced to athletics scholarships. More young men are given the opportunity to improve in this way and so raise the standard all round. Unless an American sprinter can consistently run the 100 yards in under 9·6 seconds he has no hope of reaching major competitions. If athletics scholarships were made illegal—there was a move in this direction at the 1958 meeting of the International Amateur Athletic Federation—then I believe the American set-up would suffer a crippling blow. Nearly all their best facilities are concentrated at the universities. Consequently when most athletes finish studying they normally give up their sport. They have not the British system of club athletics to the same degree.

At the Olympic Village the different nations mixed well together. The Russians had originally suggested that they would stay in their own ship instead of using the Village, but this was turned down. Rightly so because such segregation would destroy the Olympic ideal.

I think the Russians were frightened that some of their athletes might be vulnerable to non-Communistic ideas if they spent too much time in the company of Westerners. In the specialized events, like hammer-throwing, there is a brotherhood which destroys

Running for his first love—the R.A.F.—Ibbotson leads Peter Clark on a flooded track in the inter-Services Championships at Uxbridge in 1956

Wedding day—
November 6th, 1956

Below: Bred for speed—Christine, Derek and Madeleine

political barriers and for many days before the Games the top exponents of the different countries trained together. This training developed mainly into competitions between Russia and the United States, as they had the best hammer-throwers. The leading Russian, Mikhail Krivonosov, a former world-record holder, gave up the sessions because he lost so often to Harold Connolly. His withdrawal did not help; Connolly still won the Olympic title.

F

II

A letter from Kuts

I call him the British Zatopek because this lion-hearted
Huddersfield electrician is a versatile running freak, who
has still not explored his own vast, record-breaking potenti-
alities.—*Frank Rostron in the Daily Express*

IN JULY 1957—the summit of my athletics career—I received
a letter from Vladimir Kuts, the Russian who captured Olympic
gold medals for the 5,000 and 10,000 metres at Melbourne in
1956. I came third in the shorter race. This is Kuts's letter in full,
exactly as it was received:

'Dear Friends, Chataway, Pirie, Ibbotson,
          The Chairman of the Light Athletic Section of the
U.S.S.R. has acquainted me with the letter of Mr. Crump of
May 6th, 1957, in which Mr. Crump writes:
     "The British Board has heard with some surprise and sorrow
that your great Olympic champion, V. Kuts, has made a statement in *Pravda* that in the Olympic 5,000 metres, the British
athletes, Chataway, Pirie and Ibbotson, conspired together to
cause him defeat by their tactics.
     Will you please assure him that he is in error in making such
an allegation."
     I have not had opportunity to write to you in this con-
nection early as I am ill for some time.
     Now I am well. First of all, I want to assure you that I in my
interview with a correspondent of the newspaper didn't mean to
offend you, my friends, in any way.
     The matter is that the correspondent with whom I had my
interview understood me wrongly when I said that I competed

in the Olympic competitions against three outstanding English runners who were strong from the technical and tactical point of view.

Their joint run made no doubt difficult struggle with them as each of us in the course of the competition followed a tactical plan which was set before.

I have met you, friends, many times and I am sure you will not think of any premeditated step on my part against friendship which I feel is permanently set between us, and will last and develop in the future. I hope by this letter I threw a light on the question raised by Mr. Crump. I shall be grateful if you would inform Mr. Crump about this letter and convey to him my sincere regards.

Yours truly,
V. Kuts.'

There was a covering letter from Jack Crump, writing as Secretary of the British Amateur Athletic Board, to whom the letter from Kuts was originally sent. He wrote:

'Dear Derek,

I have pleasure in sending to you herewith a copy of the letter which has been sent to me by Vladimir Kuts. I have had this letter duplicated so that each of you has a copy, and I am sure you will appreciate the very excellent sentiments which Kuts expresses in it. I think it does explain the circumstances in connection with the Press reports, which were published and which caused me to write to the U.S.S.R. authorities on Kuts's alleged statements.

I think he is an extremely nice chap, and, quite obviously, from the sentiments he expresses in his letter, I think you'll share my view that he is also a great sportsman.

Yours sincerely,
J. C. J. Crump.'

Whether Kuts was quoted correctly is not the issue. Millions of Russians no doubt believed that Chataway, Pirie and myself did run as a team in an attempt to beat their national hero. I only wish this were true, because then a Briton might have won this race.

Instead there were no combined tactics—both Pirie and Chataway were confident that they could win, and had no intention of helping each other.

Both had competed in the Olympic 5,000 metres at Helsinki four years previously, and therefore had the advantage in experience. Also, they had both beaten Kuts over this distance, and at the same time set world records. In fact, Pirie had defeated the Russian that year, in the then-world-record-time of 13 min. 36.8 sec.

Pirie was upset because he had been criticized for depriving Chataway of fourth place at Helsinki. You might recall that Chataway fell at the final bend when he was in the lead. Courageously he picked himself up and continued the race. Over the last few yards Pirie overtook him, and therefore gained fourth place, with Chataway fifth. Some claimed that it was unfair of Pirie to pass the gallant Chataway. Pirie replied that he had not seen Chataway fall. Also, it must be remembered that the British, at least, believe the Olympic Games are individual events. So why should Pirie not have overtaken Chataway?

Now, four years later, they were to meet again in another Olympic Games. Once more Pirie had also run in the 10,000 metres, and a few days earlier had been crushed by Kuts, after a magnificent struggle. Pirie was the only man who tried to stay the pace with this remarkable Russian, who appeared to get a sadistic pleasure out of running his opponents into the ground.

I witnessed this race from the competitors' enclosure, and it was apparent from the expressions on many of the Russian athletes' faces that they feared Pirie might win. He ran so easily behind Kuts in the early stages, and every time the pace changed—dictated always by Kuts—Pirie closed the gap. It seemed with ease, but the spectator cannot know the agony a runner suffers. For nineteen laps this cat-and-mouse duel went on. By this time Kuts was beginning to turn round, perplexed as to whether he would ever get away from his pursuer.

Then, at the start of the twentieth lap it happened! Kuts piled on yet another of his murderous sprints. Pirie hunched his shoulders, called for another supreme effort—but his legs refused. They seemed to turn to jelly before the eyes of 100,000 spectators. This was running in its most brutal form. Only a world boxing title-fight would compare. If Pirie had been hammered to the canvas, he would not have suffered more. It was a sickening sight, only to be made worse for the British party by seeing the Russians screaming for joy. Kuts took one last look round, and knew he had conquered again.

Pirie had gambled and failed. He could have run for second or third place, but for him only victory mattered. At least he had proved the only runner who could stay with the Russian for five miles. While Kuts swept on to victory, Pirie laboured in agony over the remaining course, and was consequently overtaken by lesser athletes.

Now, five days later, he was ready to take on Kuts again. The fantastic training he had undergone in previous years had given him amazing powers of recuperation. He seemed to flower even more grandly from defeat. Revenge was his goal. He is a strange character, but an honest one. During the preparation for the Olympic Games he trained mainly alone. The Russians had watched him, clocked his times, studied his style, and many feared his ability and tenacity.

He is not easy to understand, and difficult to love. Yet it is impossible not to respect him as a runner. To Pirie athletics is a dedicated, almost monastic, life. Running has given him a power which he dreads losing.

Running has never meant as much to me, yet I took it seriously enough. That is why I was disturbed at Melbourne by the advantages others had over me. By this, I mean those who had the opportunity to travel earlier to the Olympic Games, and so prepare more meticulously. This has been well illustrated—as I have mentioned earlier —by Chris Brasher, who won the steeplechase title, and Derek Johnson, runner-up in the 800 metres. When I arrived I trained with Chataway, Brasher and Ken Wood, and realized how much they had benefited by their early arrival. Brasher was running better than ever before. In fact, I found it difficult to keep up with him in the 440-yards-interval-running spins. He even challenged me to a mile race! With Chataway and Wood also running well, I felt very much out of it all. An extra fortnight in Australia might have made all the difference.

As I have written previously, the long air journey to Australia saps away much of the fitness gained by training in England. The mind recovers before the body, and this is no doubt why I found it difficult to understand how my performances in the earlier days were so much poorer than those of the advanced party. The four of us— Chataway, Brasher, Wood and myself—liked to train on grass. So we often used a nearby race-course.

Competition is the life-blood of athletics, and therefore I wanted to accept some of the invitations offered for races before the Games. There was a two miles at Geelong, just outside Melbourne, which was won by Chris Brasher. His victory here was an indication of the greater things he was to achieve later during the Games. It gave him the confidence he needed, and I remember him saying to me: 'I think my time must be a world record for a grass track. You could only manage the same 8 min. 45·6 sec. at the fast Motspur Park Stadium.'

As this race took place only a few days after I arrived, it was out of the question for me to run. Athletes differ in regard to the value of competition during training. Chataway and Wood refused to compete at Geelong because they preferred to save everything for the Games.

To complicate my preparations, I hurt a bone in my foot on the hard track. Even when I walked it hurt. The doctor and masseur both suggested that I should have an injection before my heat of the 5,000 metres. I had vague thoughts that I would feel only one leg land, so I refused. I had never previously had an injection, and did not want to start now. Yet I did take medical advice and regretfully missed the spectacular Opening Ceremony of the Games.

When the heats for the 5,000 metres were drawn, Pirie, Chataway and I were naturally seeded in different races. After much discussion it was decided that I had the hardest race because it included Kuts.

I almost missed the start of my heat, for preceding this was the 800-metre final when Derek Johnson ran such a gallant race, to lose a gold medal only by a mere eighteen inches. For most of the race the coloured American Arnie Sowell was in the lead. On the final bend the favourite, Tom Courtney, also of the U.S.A., made his challenge. He was so impatient that he swung wide coming into the final straight, and Derek Johnson slipped inside. As Sowell faded, Johnson found himself in the lead. You can imagine the excitement of the British as Johnson led down the final straight. Twenty yards from the finish I thought he would win. Then the powerful American, Courtney, galvanized his huge frame and lunged at the tape just before Derek could finish with upright body in true English style. And during the English season Johnson had been showing poor form! He is one of the most talented athletes I have ever met, and no doubt he was helped by travelling to Melbourne early.

When I went on to the track, I saw Kuts, whom I had never met, and said, ''Ow do?' Obviously he did not understand Yorkshire.

I had no fears about qualifying, but ran the first two miles fast, and then let the leaders go away, thinking only of finishing in the first five. Alan Lawrence, the Australian who was third in the 10,000 metres, wasted his energy, in my opinion, in an all-out effort to beat Kuts. His 'success' received great praise in the Australian Press. Most Australian sports writers seem to know little about athletics because they assumed that those who won heats in fast times would obviously be favourites in the final. This, of course, is illogical as a runner like Chataway delights in qualifying in the slowest time possible. Personally, I think a fastish time sharpens up the muscles for the final, but this does not mean that it is necessary to go all out to win a heat. It might have been important to Lawrence to do so, because it gave the Australian spectators something to cheer about. I found that the Olympic crowd were generally poor sports, intent on cheering only their own countrymen. Australia has a great reputation in the world of sport, and their spectators should now be big enough to appreciate fine performances by competitors of other countries.

A few hours before the 5,000-metre final I went into Pirie's room at the Olympic Village to discuss the race. He was relaxing on his bed, and greeted me with a jaunty grin.

'What's the plan for the afternoon, Gordon?' I asked.

'I think I can beat Kuts again because he lacks speed at the finish,' Pirie answered. 'But I warn you the man we must think about is Chataway. In my view Chataway is the man we have to watch.'

Even from Pirie, with his reputation for frankness, this was an astonishing statement. I had come to talk about tactics, feeling very much the small member of the team, and here was Pirie telling me that the important thing was to watch another British runner. The rivalry between Pirie and Chataway had been smouldering for years, which was only natural as they were two of the greatest 5,000-metre runners in the world.

All the time I trained with Chataway he had never discussed the race which had brought us both 12,000 miles. Whether he felt like Pirie, I do not know. All I can say is that my talk with Pirie shattered me. A few nights before I had thought of a plan which I considered might give Britain the gold medal in the 5,000 metres. If it had been operated, the Russian allegation would have been correct—we would have used tactics. As it was the Russian suggestion was awry.

I myself was not over-confident about victory, just hoping for the best. Maybe that was why I could anticipate the race more objectively. In my view Britain was represented by three runners, all of whom had a chance of winning, but this could only be achieved if Kuts were mastered. My plan was to allow Kuts to lead early, and so break up the field before the half-way stage. It was important for the British runners to stay together on his tail so we could then work together for a British victory. I was convinced it would not have been difficult for any one of us to move into the lead ahead of Kuts, and then another of us to run by his side, with the third following up in the rear. By this method Kuts would have been boxed in and forced to run at our pace. This would have been a tremendous psychological blow to a man who loves to be out on his own, so that he can execute his murderous sprints to break the hearts and lungs of those who try to trail him. To add to his discomfort, we could change the lead when we liked, with Pirie, Chataway and myself alternating. This would mean that we could keep the pace more even and wait until the last 800 metres for the 'kill'.

It was generally accepted that Pirie, Chataway and I all had faster finishes, so that it would not mean that one would make a sacrifice for the other, because victory would depend on the man with the most speed at the end. If Kuts had won against these tactics, then he would have proved himself a supreme Olympic champion.

Some people might think it unfair to use strength of numbers to win an Olympic race, but I know of many countries that do not have the same scruples. The Finnish pre-war supremacy in distance running was built up mainly because of their tactics. Also, it was to the credit of Britain that they and Russia were the only countries who had managed to get three men in the final. The other two Russian competitors, Bolotnikov and Chernyavskiy, were never in the race, and therefore could not have been of any assistance to Kuts in stopping such a British plan.

We travelled to the Olympic Stadium together, accompanied by Leslie Truelove, the assistant British team manager. During the journey Truelove talked about the breeding of chickens—no doubt to take our minds off the race.

Pirie and I both sneaked out on the track to try it out when we went to the start. Kuts's face gave no indication of his feelings. He was completely absorbed in his own thoughts, and moved mechanically to the starting-line. The Olympic Stadium was full. Everyone wanted to know whether Kuts could emulate the mighty Zatopek by adding the 5,000-metre crown to the 10,000-metre title he had won five days previously. The other questions which would be solved before the end of this race were whether Gordon Pirie was going to avenge his 10,000-metre defeat, and if Chataway was still the track's 'Red Fox'.

The line-up for the race was as follows: Vladimir Kuts (Russia), Pyotr Bolotnikov (Russia), Ivan Chernyavskiy (Russia), Laszlo Tabori (Hungary), Miklos Szabo (Hungary), Albert Thomas (Australia), Nyandika Maiyoro (Kenya), Thygbe Thorgersen (Denmark), Herbert Schade (Germany), Bill Dellinger (U.S.A.), Velisa Mugosa (Yugoslavia), Gordon Pirie (Britain), Chris Chataway (Britain), Derek Ibbotson (Britain).

As expected Kuts was in the lead within half a lap. Pirie followed in his wake. I had great confidence in Gordon's ability, and decided to stick by him. So I tucked behind in third position. For the first few laps the whole field clung together, but soon Kuts's furious pace began to tell, and before the half-way stage the field had been scattered into groups. Pirie was second, I was third and Chataway fourth, while some forty yards behind the Hungarian Tabori was leading another section of runners. So it was Kuts versus Britain, at least from the stand, unfortunately not in fact as I have explained previously.

I realized that it would be fatal to let Kuts get away, and this made it easier to keep up the fierce pace set. Anyway, it was not faster than Iharos in Budapest. After about two miles Chataway moved up to second position behind Kuts. I could not understand why he should do this because normally he is happier in the rear of the leading group. We were later to discover that he was in serious trouble with stomach cramp, and had closed up in the hope of killing off the pain. But after 200 yards in this position, Pirie and I witnessed the depressing sight of Kuts drawing away. Chataway was unable to go with him, and for three vital seconds Pirie dithered. By the time he decided to move after the Russian it was too late. Kuts had escaped, and we were never to catch him again. I felt almost sick with disappointment, and wished I had sensed the danger early and gone up. Instead, I had a blind faith in Gordon. Until then the race had provided me with no difficulty. Afterwards Pirie blamed Chataway for losing contact, but I did not agree with this. Chris had been in trouble before this stage in the race, although unknown to us.

For almost a lap Pirie and I strove in vain to catch up with the Russian, while Chataway fell back pathetically and finished eleventh. Kuts reached the bell, commanding a lead of fifty yards which meant that only an accident could prevent him from winning. I was then in second place, and content to fight it out with Pirie for the silver medal. There was no point in chasing Kuts, and as the other runners were a long way behind, neither of us was in a desperate hurry.

We both entered the final straight as Kuts lifted his arms in triumph, ninety yards away. At this moment Pirie sped past me, and sadly I had no answer. Even so, I finished an easy third, and won the bronze medal.

After the Victory Ceremony Kuts showed Pirie his medal, and I sneaked up from behind and grabbed it. I darted across the arena, and Kuts seemed worried that he might lose his proud possession, so I called off the joke.

Thus I had a gold medal—for ten seconds.

12

Dawn of great events

The reason for his phenomenal success is no secret. Derek Ibbotson brings a laughing, uninhibited outlook to his sport. He loves and lives for running. No running robot, he is the gay cavalier of British sport.—*Roy Moor*, *News Chronicle*

SIX days before I returned home from the Olympic Games at Melbourne, Madeleine found a flat, thanks to Eddie Lacey, a Press photographer. Dear Madeleine had little sleep during this period of getting everything ready for us to start married life. We had married only a few days before I left for Australia.

At the homecoming luncheon for the British team, at the Lancaster Court Hotel, I managed to steel myself against eating as Madeleine had warned me she was preparing *our* first meal—and she had got up at 4.30 in the morning—after two hours' sleep—to start it! She passed with flying honours, thanks to soup, fried chicken, bread sauce, brussels sprouts, peas, roast and boiled potatoes, fresh fruit and cream, sherry and table wine.

After a few days at our new home in Mitcham, I returned to Yatesbury, the R.A.F. station full of happy memories, to be demobbed. The Commanding Officer called me to his office to say goodbye. It was sad to take off my uniform for the last time. This was the end of a wonderful period of my life. For two years I had had no worries about holding a job, and every facility possible was made available for those who wanted to pursue a sporting career.

At Yatesbury they even built a water-jump to help one of my friends, Dave Shaw, a steeplechaser. No wonder the R.A.F. had twenty representatives in the British Olympic team at Melbourne. No wonder I continued to wear the blue running-vest of the Service.

Madeleine and I spent Christmas with my parents at Huddersfield. Then again I had to say *au revoir* to Yorkshire to start work as a junior sales representative with W. T. Henley's Telegraph Works, Ltd., in London.

It was uncertain where I would work in the future so I regretfully resigned from Longwood Harriers, and joined South London Harriers. This move was forced on me by the A.A.A. rule which prevents a runner competing in senior competition unless he is a first-claim member of his club, and Longwood Harriers entered only for the Northern tournaments. I successfully appealed to the Hard Cases Committee of the Southern Counties Committee so that I could run first-claim for South London Harriers without waiting the required fourteen months.

The following year when I found myself back living and working in Yorkshire I was unable to rejoin Longwood Harriers as a first-claim member without resigning from South London Harriers and serving the waiting period. This would have meant missing the Area and National cross-country championships. On the other hand, as I was not a member of a Yorkshire club, I was not allowed to compete in the Yorkshire Championships. Such is the bureaucracy of athletics.

These laws were formed many years ago to prevent poaching of athletes from one club to another. As far as I know, there is little danger of this these days. Surely it is time to bring the rules up to date?

South London Harriers is one of the greatest clubs in Britain, and produces an endless stream of premier distance runners. Since the war, these have included Gordon Pirie, Laurie Reed, Mike Firth and Peter Driver.

Due to the Olympic Games, I missed my usual basic winter training for cross-country running, but still managed to come fourteenth in the Inter-Counties Championships, and the same position in an international race at Hannaut, Belgium. Then I finished third in the Southern, and sixth in the National Championships, which indicated a return to form. I was chosen for the England team at the international in Brussels that year, but owing to tonsillitis I was unable to compete.

I had been invited to run in the U.S.A. indoor meetings early in 1957, but this was turned down as the Americans could not afford to pay for a British team manager as well. It would not have been so annoying if officialdom always insisted on sending a team manager, but there have been many cases where the rule has been waived to suit British officials.

When Roger Bannister, McDonald Bailey and Arthur Wint competed in New Zealand, they travelled alone half-way across the world without a manager. But to conform to Britain's rigid rules, Bannister was made team manager, Wint captain and McDonald Bailey vice-captain of a three-man team. This sort of thing just makes a farce of regulations which, anyway, are farcical in themselves. Most experienced athletes are quite capable of looking after themselves in foreign countries.

I did get indoor competitions, however, as two meetings were organized by the Mancastrian Club at Belle Vue, Manchester. A remarkable technical operation was needed to make a track and seats were lifted from the middle of the auditorium to provide space. It meant running between rows of spectators which was a strange experience. Admittedly, it seemed a Heath Robinson affair, but at least it was more realistic than the dream of an indoor track which Britain has been cherishing since the war.

The meeting created a record which may never be beaten—a 'mile' in 3 min. 37·4 sec.—20·6 seconds faster than the world record held at the time by John Landy, of Australia.

The small field included Ken Wood and Brian Hewson—both Olympic 1,500-metre finalists—and myself. Brian was in great condition, and went straight into the lead, to avoid the bumping which might occur on such a small track. He soon led by ten yards, which meant Wood and myself had almost lost contact. The pace seemed fantastic, and I felt as if I was on a fairground scenic railway. To get advantage of the inside bend, I ran dangerously close to the spectators. We were lapping the 120-yard track at about sixteen to seventeen seconds. During the race I wondered whether the officials had left out a lap, though it was such a bizarre experience nothing seemed to make much sense. Wood and I tried to increase our pace but we could not catch the graceful Hewson. A few laps from the end Hewson began to tire—and started to come back to us. Wood swung to the outside, and Brian had nothing left. So the race was now between two Yorkshiremen—Ken and myself. As overtaking was dangerous, I decided to leave my effort until the end. With

about twenty yards to go, I began to make a wide circuit around
Wood. Maybe it was the slope or Ken's elbow, I do not know, but
just when I thought victory was mine, I was sent sprawling on the
hard boards. Wood won, and his time was announced at 3 min.
37·4 sec., with mine 3 min. 38·6 sec.

Afterwards it was discovered we had run 138 yards short of a
mile. Nevertheless, the winning time would have been equivalent
to something under the world indoor record of 4 min. 3·6 sec.,
held at the time by Gunnar Nielsen of Denmark.

The next time I ran in a similar meeting Brian Hewson was again
in the race. In the dressing-room we decided to put on a show and
agreed to lead on alternate laps. Brian must have changed his mind,
because I ended up leading all the way. Even so, I held him at the
finish and won in 4 min. 7 sec., compared to his 4 min. 7·2 sec.

Indoor tracks are essential for athletics. Primarily they help the
sprinters and certain field-events competitors, but can also be of
great assistance to middle-distance runners, especially those who
do not take part in cross-country events. To remain in international
class, it is necessary to train throughout the year, and this can become
tedious during the winter without the incentive of competition.
In 1956 I.T.V. offered British athletics an indoor track, but for some
unknown reason this offer was refused.

Meetings of this sort have been held in the U.S.A. for many years,
and I am convinced this is one of the prime reasons for America
dominating the sprints. Russia and Germany have followed this
lead, and now hold a prominent position in European athletics.
What is more, indoor athletics can be a tremendous box-office
draw, and so provide financial benefits to the sport.

A sports arena such as Wembley would be ideal, but nobody
appears willing to find the few thousand pounds needed to provide
a track. While the authority of British athletics remains in so few
hands, progress inevitably will be slow.

I am convinced the Manchester indoor meetings helped considerably to lay the foundations of the successes I was to achieve
during the summer of 1957. It was the same for Ken Wood, who later
ran the mile in 3 min. 59·3 sec., when I broke the world record. Brian
Hewson was handicapped by injuries, so it was not possible to
judge the beneficial effects of indoor running on him.

My first outdoor meeting was at the Leyton Floodlit Sports,

where I competed over 1,500 metres and won in 3 min. 47·8 sec.—the same time as Jack Lovelock recorded when winning the Olympic title in 1936 at Berlin.

Then it was a world record, but times had changed. It did not seem particularly fast.

I followed this by a couple of mile races and I beat Peter Driver and Mike Berisford. My intensive training during the early months of the year was beginning to tell. My next important race was at the Oxford University v. A.A.A. meeting at Iffley Road. It was on the corresponding evening in 1954 that Roger Bannister had made history by crashing the four-minute mile. This all seemed the perfect setting to prove I was a miler to be reckoned with. Even the weather conditions were similar to those on Bannister's great night. John McDonald, a Westcountryman whom I knew in the R.A.F., was competing for the A.A.A. and we agreed that it would be to the advantage of our team if we made the pace fast. Among the Oxford University representatives was Derek Johnson, a brilliant half-miler who had had a certain amount of success over the mile.

McDonald agreed to run the first lap in the lead, and I would take over until the half-mile. Lap times of 59·2 seconds and 61·2 seconds followed, but I was impatient and took over before the three-quarter mile mark, which was passed in 3 min. 1·8 sec. The pace had not broken the field and I was worried about Johnson. So I eased over the first furlong of the last lap. But when I decided to sprint, Johnson failed to come with me and I won in 4 min. 0·6 sec. If I had sprinted all-out from 500 yards, I would have broken four minutes again.

The Oxford race gave me the confidence I needed for the trip to Los Angeles a week later. Brian Hewson was to be my partner in a much-publicized mile. The trip was officially sanctioned this time and we had Jack Crump as team manager. He had arranged for us to stay a couple of days at Cleveland, Ohio, to get acclimatized. I wrote and suggested that it would be better to go straight to Los Angeles so as to have a longer rest from travelling before the race.

But we stopped at Cleveland. This meant that we arrived in Los Angeles only two days before the race, while, in contrast, Merv Lincoln, of Australia, our main rival, had already been there three days. In my view it is an advantage to be in the city where a race takes place, as long as possible.

It has often been said that I talk too much, especially to the Press. I did this in Los Angeles when I said it was my intention to lead all the way and win.

It was a colourful meeting, including many relays. The ten times 100 yards race is a spectacle seldom seen in Europe, and one of the reasons why the U.S.A. has such an abundance of front-ranking sprinters.

Tom Courtney, the Olympic 800-metre champion, whom I met in Melbourne, broke the world half-mile record with a time of 1 min. 46·8 sec., and this whetted the appetite of the 40,000 crowd for the mile. As in Britain, the four-lap race is the *pièce de résistance* of an athletics meeting, like the world heavyweight championship in boxing. The field included Laszlo Tabori, the Hungarian refugee, Hewson, Lincoln and a number of American runners. At the start Lincoln got down like a sprinter, and I joked, 'Don't you find it cold down there?'

Hewson led for the first fifty yards, but then I took over, set on my plan of running away from the field in Kuts style. It didn't work out like that. At the half-way stage they were still with me, and I knew I had made a tactical error. I slowed down the third lap to leave myself something in reserve. There was no change in the order until the final bend when Lincoln challenged. I was not prepared for this at the bend, and found myself boxed in. When at last I was free to move, Lincoln, Hewson and Tabori were in front, and this remained the order until the tape. Why can't I keep my big mouth shut before a race?

The next evening Brian and myself went to Modesto, in California, to compete at another meeting. This was a fabulous carnival of athletics which went on from noon until midnight. I again ran in the mile. Although Lincoln was also entered, I could not find him when the twenty-eight runners lined up. This time I had decided to make him lead, but was still frightened that I would come out in front when the field broke up. Fortunately, I spotted Lincoln, and had no difficulty in moving with him when he began a long sprint to the tape. I gained my revenge. The value of that extra day in California was again underlined when Brian Hewson won the 800-metre race convincingly, beating the famous Olympic coloured runner, Arnie Sowell, in a time of under 1 min. 50 sec.

13

The purple patch

Derek Ibbotson compensated dramatically for his mile
fluff by breaking the British three-mile record in a race
which caused thousands of spectators at the White City to
rush the rails in the pouring rain and cheer him home in one
of his greatest performances.—*J. L. Manning, Sunday
Dispatch*

LIKE a gambler's lucky streak, everyone at some period in his life
hits a fleeting spell when everything goes right for him. My
golden days came just after my return to England. I became the
father of a beautiful daughter and that inspired me to a run of
success beyond all my dreams. From June 8th to August 17th of
1957 I ran the mile three times under four minutes, captured the
world record, and replaced Chris Chataway as holder of the British
three-mile record. Of twenty-seven races, I won all but three—and
in those I was second.

My first important engagement after returning from Los Angeles
was the international mile during the Whitsun British Games at
the White City, London.

The Los Angeles race had taught me the folly of front running
in a class mile field and the presence of Klaus Richtzenhain, from
East Germany, was a further warning that a more canny approach
was needed. Richtzenhain had come through with a dynamic sprint
in the Olympic 1,500 metres at Melbourne the previous year to win
the silver medal.

He did not relish the role of pace-maker but as so often happens
in this type of race he was not given the choice.

After an opening lap of 60·1 seconds he seemed anxious for me,
running second, to take over and he slowed the next quarter to

almost 64 seconds. I refused to take the bait, satisfied to run quietly in his wake. The third quarter was also slow, and he reached the bell in 3 min. 7·1 sec. At last Richtzenhain began to increase the pace. I remained within a yard of his swift, lithe body, full of confidence. Down the back-straight he looked round anxiously. My surprise gave way to the sudden realization that I had him 'cooked'. As I reached his shoulder he surrendered so tamely that I felt almost disappointed. A final lap of 56 seconds gave me a twenty-five-yard victory in 4 min. 3·2 sec.

When warming-down I remembered a letter which had been waiting for me in the dressing-room. I had not had time to read it before the race and had stuffed it in my track-suit pocket. I read: 'We are very pleased to see you are going back north. We are fed up with your big head and boastful manner. You'll never be as good a sportsman as Chris Chataway.' This was signed by thirty athletics fans from Wembley.

It hurt me to read such a letter and I momentarily resolved to try and curb my natural exuberance, which had so often been interpreted as conceit. But what was the use, I wasn't the type to assume the silent shroud of modesty that so often covers even bigger heads than mine.

That evening I flew to Holland as a guest-runner with the Mitcham Athletic Club, and the next day ran in a 1,500 metres. A septic leg prevented me from bending my knee, and I could only manage a slow time of 3 min. 57 sec. for second place. Before returning home I successfully ran three more races in Holland.

The following Saturday I was in Glasgow, to compete at the Police Sports at Ibrox Park. During the morning I went out shopping, and on my return to the hotel where the English team were staying, all the boys greeted me by singing 'O Mein Papa'.

That was how I discovered that Madeleine had given birth to a daughter that morning. Immediately I phoned my wife at the Carshalton Hospital. 'Now, we expect you to run a good race to celebrate,' she said.

I usually had a sleep before a big race, but I was so excited that I could not relax. I kept on thinking how splendid it would be if I could break the world record on the day Christine was born. Before the start of the mile some of the British competitors offered to set the pace.

Les Locke, a Scottish Empire Games runner who later played professional football for Queen's Park Rangers, opened the race with a first lap of 57·2 seconds. Then the South African, Paul Soine, took over the lead. I was so anxious to stay up that I ran too close to Soine, and was spiked, but managed to go through the half-mile mark at 1 min. 58 sec. Now, if I could beat two minutes in the next half of the race, the world record would be mine! The thought of celebrating Christine's birth with such a triumph urged me to take the lead with 600 yards still to run.

With the temperature near the nineties it was like running in an oven. The heat was coming off the cinders and I was almost choked with dust. No wonder I did not hear the three-quarter-mile time of 2 min. 59·8 sec. There was no challenge but the good-natured Scottish crowd urged me on as I ran alone over the last part of the race. At the end I was completely exhausted and could not speak until I had had a shandy. I will always remember this as one of the toughest races of my career.

The time of 3 min. 58·4 sec. was four-tenths of a second outside Landy's record but ranked me number two miler in the world. It was better than Laszlo Tabori's European and British All-Comers' record of 3 min. 59 sec.

Down in Carshalton the nurses told Madeleine that they had heard on the radio that I had broken the record. 'Which record?' she asked. No one knew, so they sent out for an evening paper.

There was no aircraft leaving Glasgow for London that evening so I had to wait until Sunday before I could see Madeleine and Christine. Press photographers were waiting at the hospital when I arrived, and they took shots of me running past a signpost which said, 'Go slow—5 miles per hour limit'. When I saw my daughter for the first time I wondered whether she would be a great runner. With fond paternal foolishness I had a good look at her limbs and decided that here was a world-beater in the making. Madeleine said she was the image of me—the usual sop for the proud father.

At that time I was living and working in Huddersfield, which meant I did not see Madeleine and Christine again until the following Wednesday when I came to London to run the two miles in the Air Ministry sports. I overstayed my time at the hospital and then was caught in a traffic jam at Hammersmith. I jumped in a taxi to the White City, and changed into my track gear on the way.

When I reached the stadium the two miles was due to start within five minutes so I had little time to warm-up. The field included Gordon Pirie, whom I had never beaten. I felt this was my big chance and went straight into the lead to get my body warm. The other runners were delighted that I set the pace, but I was confident and sensed that this was one of those occasions when I could afford to take the risk.

In the past whenever I had run against Pirie I had never been able to break away. This time it was different. Over the last lap, when I began to sprint, he failed to come with me. I just romped home, and looked back to see him ten yards behind. Then I remembered the debt I owed to the man I had beaten. I had always admired Gordon. He had helped me a great deal, and was prepared to discuss his ideas on training. It was never quite the same with Chataway, and that's why I gained more personal satisfaction in beating the 'Red Fox'. As an athlete Chataway was a mystery to me. He never appeared prepared to pool ideas.

At this time I became involved in yet another controversy. Promoters in Dublin and Darlington both claimed I was due to run at their meetings on Monday, June 24th. I had accepted the Dublin invitation forgetting that earlier in the season I had tentatively agreed to run in Darlington. I receive so many invitations to run at meetings all over the country that it is not always easy to keep a check.

It was suggested that I did not want to run in Dublin, but preferred Darlington to avoid meeting Ron Delany, the Irish Olympic champion. The row became so heated that eventually it was sorted out by two leading officials, Jack Crump and Les Truelove. They agreed that, as I had accepted the Darlington invitation first, I must run there.

To illustrate how tied up I was, I forgot to send my entry form in for the Northern Counties mile race. As I wanted to compete in the Area Championships, I defended my three-mile title, the holder being entered automatically. I was delighted to discover that all the mile running I was doing had not affected my stamina, and I was still able to win this race by sixty yards, in 13 min. 37 sec. The same day I ran a mile race and won in 4 min. 12·4 sec. It often surprises people that I compete in so many small meetings. The answer is that I love competitive running, and I find small races a relief from the more important ones.

Above: The price of fame. Ibbotson besieged by young autograph hunters. *Below:* It's never too late. Laszlo Tabori believes that victory is his in the London-Budapest match at the White City, 1956. But that mighty Ibbotson chest is just about to lift the tape first

Above: Soon after the start of the Olympic 5,000 metres at the Melbourne Olympics. Tabori (Hungary) and Kuts (Russia) lead from Britain's trio, Pirie, Ibbotson, Chataway

Right: 'All that glisters . . .' Ibbotson had to be content with a bronze medal in the above event. He receives it from Mr. Avory Brundage, chief of the Games Committee, as Gordon Pirie and the fabulous Vladimir Kuts look on

London is not the only athletics centre. If interest in the sport is to be stimulated, the up-country meetings must be supported.

In 1957 I entered for the A.A.A. mile championship for the first time. My form was so good that I had high hopes of winning the title. In fact, I told my friends to look out for me in the race on television. What a shock it was when *I did not even make the final*!

Arriving in London on the Friday, I went over to Feltham to see Madeleine and Christine. Once again, I stayed too long. I rushed to the White City in a taxi, changing into running-kit as I went, and on arrival I had only five minutes to prepare. Like a car engine the body needs warming-up if it is going to perform well. Most people consider they are out of condition if they find themselves puffing and panting after running for a bus. But the fittest athlete is affected in this way. It is just another proof of the importance of getting the body ready before stern exercise.

Ideally I like at least half an hour to warm-up, followed by a short rest in the dressing-room and a few sprints before the race.

I have never understood why other sportsmen do not take the same care in preparation. It is not good enough for footballers just to kick the ball about. An early goal can often be conceded before the reflexes are tuned to maximum effort. Despite failing to adhere to these firm convictions, I thought I could comfortably finish in the first three of my heat and so qualify for the final the next day. It was a slow race, and everything seemed too easy. On the last lap the Scot, Graham Everett, started to sprint like mad. At first I could not understand why he was in such a hurry because a runner of his class was in little danger of not qualifying. Then I remembered that it was not the first three, but only the winners and fastest losers who reached the final.

I realized then I had to win, and went after Everett. But it was too late and I finished second in 4 min. 15·5 sec., and had to wait anxiously until the next two heats were completed to know whether I had qualified. I was the seventh-fastest loser and missed the final by 0·1 second.

It was my own fault, but I felt a bit of a mug having told my friends to look in on television and see me in the mile. And I was annoyed with the time-qualifying system. In the Olympic Games and other major events the heats are seeded and qualification for the final depends on where you finish, not your time.

I was not the only one to suffer that evening. Mike Farrell, who came fifth in the 800 metres at the Melbourne Olympic Games, did not reach the final qualifiers for the half-mile. He was drawn in the same heat as the Irishman, Ron Delany, and it was a tactical race with Delany winning over the last fifty yards. Many great runners, like Lovelock, Wooderson and Bannister, to mention just a few, had won the A.A.A. mile title, and I was dead keen to add my name to the roll. Now my chance had gone.

That evening I was so irritable that Madeleine exploded: 'Why don't you forget about athletics? You're getting like Gordon Pirie.'

'Forget? How can I?' I answered. 'Here I am the fastest current miler in the world, and I'm not even good enough to get into the British championship mile final.'

'Well, you have your chance in the three miles tomorrow,' she said.

'It's not the same. I wanted to win the mile title. Anyway, the three miles will not be good for me because I am running against Ron Delany and Stanislav Jungwirth in a mile next Friday. The extra distance might affect my speed.'

'Well, you don't have to run,' she retorted shortly.

'Don't have to run!' I almost shouted. 'I've not only got to run, I've got to set a record to show I'm not all washed up.'

Before going to sleep I worked out the lap times to aim at in the three miles. Two years previously I had done this to help Chris Chataway set a world record of 13 min. 23·2 sec. Now I was out to break this time myself, though it was no longer a world record as the Hungarian, Sandor Iharos, had since achieved a time of 13 min. 14·2 sec. This was a little too good for me as I had not trained for the three miles that season. Chataway's British record would satisfy me.

Before going to the White City on the Saturday, Madeleine and I went shopping. One character in the market offered me a ticket for the Championships, saying, 'I wouldn't like you to miss the mile altogether.'

That was the bitter end. I just had to do something really good.

It was raining heavily at the start of the three miles, and I rather like running in the rain, especially in the longer races. The West Country runner, Dennis Crook, opened the race with a fast lap of 61 seconds. This was excellent, and set my body into the right

tempo for a fast race. Crook kept the pace up, and it was a consolation to know I did not feel the strain of running the longer distance.
At the half-way stage the pace became too slow for me, and I went
away by myself, thinking only of Chataway's record. At two miles in
8 min. 50·8 sec. I held a lead of seventy yards, and was well inside
the record schedule.

All my anger at failing to qualify for the mile was being put to
good use in my running. With every stride I felt I was digging my
spikes into those who had taunted me. Wiping mud from my eyes
and feeling drenched suited my mood of revenge and atonement.

Over the last mile I tired a little, but still produced a final last
lap of 63 seconds, and was overjoyed when I heard the time was
13 min. 20·8 secs.—2·4 seconds inside Chataway's record. I had
beaten my nearest rival by 150 yards, and everyone forgave me my
humiliating flop in the mile.

14

Perpetual motion

How do you run—let alone win—a two-mile race with the ball of your foot rubbed away into a giant, raw, glistening blister? You don't—unless your name is Derek Ibbotson, and you own a fantastic brand of courage.—*Harry Carpenter, Daily Mail*

I FELT very pleased with life after the A.A.A. Championships, and would have had little regret if this had been the end of the season. In fact, we were only at the half-way stage, and within six days I was due to face the fastest middle-distance field ever assembled on a British track. This was the race which marked the summit of my whole career—the breaking of the world mile record. I have already told you of the race in an earlier chapter. Now we come to the hectic days which followed. A wise man would have taken a rest, but wisdom has never been my strong point. I find it impossible to copy the clinical approach to running of Roger Bannister. He always ensured himself a number of weeks' rest between races. Before breaking the world record, which had been completely unplanned, I had committed myself to run three times within the following five days. In the headlines they called me 'The Wonder Runner' and 'Non-Stop Ibbotson'. Twelve hours after clocking my 3 min. 57·2 sec. mile I was touring a Tyneside shipyard, and later competing at Hebburn in a two-mile race in the Hawthorn Leslie's Sports. The meeting took place in torrential rain, and although I felt very tired I managed to win. Of course, I should have taken a short holiday but I had promised to run again on the Monday at Berwick-on-Tweed.

As 5,000 people had turned out and got soaked at Hebburn, I could hardly let down those who expected me to appear in Berwick.

At that meeting, I discovered later, bookmakers were offering odds of 3 to 1 against my running the mile in under four minutes. I hope nobody accepted the odds because I had strained the tendons in my left leg. My winning time was 10·2 seconds outside four minutes. In the old days, I am told, illegal betting was common in athletics, but this was the first time I had known it happen at a meeting in which I competed.

My winning time might have been faster if the opposition had been better, but Ken Wood, who was originally down to run, wired the promoters that he was not available. This meant he would be fresh when we met at Manchester two days later. I suppose I too could have withdrawn, but I felt under an obligation. I visited the Newcastle United Football Club ground to receive massage treatment for my leg from trainer Norman Smith. Two of the Newcastle stars, Jackie Milburn and Jimmy Scoular, were friends of mine.

Some of the players asked about my preparations before running the world record. I gave them an outline of my training and suggested it might be a good thing if footballers did more basic exercise instead of concentrating mainly on ball-work. English football, I consider, will not reassert its supremacy until old-fashioned methods are replaced by modern ideas. It is strange that amateur sports like swimming and athletics readily accept the new approach while professional sports, such as boxing and football, continue with the attitude: 'We did it in the old days, so it must still be good enough.'

The meeting at Manchester was organized by the Mancastrian Club and included most of the American athletes who had appeared for New York against London at London's White City the previous week-end.

Many of them were Olympic champions, but to the 12,000 spectators the mile was still the main event. They wanted to see a race of under four minutes, as Ken Wood and myself, who had beaten that time the previous Friday, were competing. This was my fourth race in six days, and my leg was still troubling me, so I was not thinking about records. I commented, 'I understand the mile prize is a pair of crutches, in case I win.'

There is only a small track at the White City, Manchester, and five laps have to be covered for a mile, which is not helpful to a fast time.

Les Locke, the Scottish Empire Games half-miler, agreed to make the early pace. He did not seem to be moving well, and twice I urged him, 'Faster, faster.' After only two laps he dropped out with stitch and I had to go it alone. This was a gamble with Ken Wood hovering in the background.

When there was only a furlong left and Wood still had not challenged, I felt safe. My peace of mind was suddenly shattered, as Wood rushed past and opened up an eight-yard gap.

I was tempted to give him best, but in a split-second my will to win regained its power and I went off after him. I was at his shoulder at the final bend, and somehow had enough energy left to fling myself past him to win by a few yards in 4 min. 3·3 sec. Both my legs were pouring blood where Wood had accidentally spiked me. It was one of the most exhausting races I had experienced as I almost lost the desire to win. An ambulance man treated me with iodine, which, in my exhausted condition, caused me to scream with pain.

The next day most of the newspapers reported Wood as saying:

'I'll show Ibbotson when I'm fit. I've beaten him eighteen times out of twenty, and I thought I had him again tonight —but my long rest from running has let me down. Just give me another two months of training, and we'll see who's the faster.'

These comments did not disturb me. I admire a forthright expression of fighting spirit and have never been an exponent of diplomatic politeness myself. I did not understand his figures as we had met no more than ten times.

However, Wood sent me the following letter:

'Dear Derek,
        Just a few lines to let you know my comments on what the newspapers wrote after yesterday's mile race.
    I hope you don't believe all the tripe they printed, but I can assure you that I didn't say anything about showing you the next time we meet. I have always been a great admirer of you, Derek, and hope we always remain the best of friends. Of course, I know that you will realize that the newspapers put in anything to fill a column.
    All the best to you and family,
                                        Ken Wood.'

But I had other worries, as the following Monday I was due to meet Ron Delany over a mile in Dublin. This was my first visit to the Irish capital, and I was overwhelmed with hospitality. It was amusing to be approached in the street by complete strangers who said, 'We wish you the best of luck, but hope Ronnie thrashes you.' All very Irish and all very friendly.

The promoter was Billy Morton, one of the most colourful personalities in athletics administration. He is a small man, with a shock of grey hair, and a great talker. In his younger days Billy was a marathon runner, and now he spends most of his time helping Irish athletics.

It was his drive and personality which made it possible in 1958 to build Ireland's first cinder track, where Herb Elliott and Albert Thomas broke three world records—over one, two and three miles. This has naturally encouraged the view that this is a super track. I agree it is one of the best in the world. No wonder Britain could do with a Morton.

This track was not in existence then and the meeting was held at the Rugby stadium, Lansdowne Road, on a grass track, which is always slower than cinders. There were a couple of pace-makers, Paul Toomy and Harry Thomas, but they went off so fast that it would have been crazy to follow them. This meant there were two races—one between Toomy and Thomas and the other between Peter Clark, Delany and myself. Before we passed the half-mile in 2 min. 2 sec., Toomy and Thomas had fallen behind to continue their personal duel.

I realized that the pace was not fast enough to sap Delany's finish and asked Clark, a former R.A.F. chum of mine, whether he could pep it up a bit. He could not respond, and I would have been wiser to take the lead then. As it was we passed the three-quarter-mile mark in 3 min. 9 sec., which meant I was a sitting target for Delany's sprint finish. This was the Irish Olympic champion's first race since I had beaten him in the world record mile ten days previously.

My only course was to sprint from the bell. This surprised Delany but he soon caught up with me, and won an exciting race over the last fifty yards. I felt no disgrace at being beaten by such a great athlete as Delany.

My miling achievements did not influence the British selectors who named me for the three miles against France. Perhaps it was advantageous to the team for me to run over the longer distance. Laurie Reed, a tall South London Harrier who had been coached by Gordon Pirie, whom he resembled, was my partner. It was his first international and I ran a 'team race' to help him along to ensure maximum points for Britain.

There was to be an international against Russia later in the month, and I was hoping to run in the 5,000 metres against Vladimir Kuts. Therefore the race against France provided excellent preparation.

During the race one of my spikes broke so it was a good thing the pace was not fast.

After winning I found my foot was badly blistered, and by the following Monday could hardly walk. I was advised to withdraw from the international two miles, and intended to do so. But when I arrived at the White City, there was a crowd of 30,000 and it seemed wrong to let them down. Having received treatment from the British team masseur, Len Kilby, and a pain-killing injection, my foot felt better and I decided to run.

My chief rival was the twenty-one-year-old Polish soldier, Kris Zimny. The Finchley runner, Frank Salvat, stayed with us for the first mile (4 min. 16·8 sec.) and then it became a straight race between Zimny and myself. The Polish runner was in the lead, and I was happy to let him stay there—but with half a mile left the effect of the injection had worn off, and each time I put my foot down pain darted up my leg. I decided to get the race over as quickly as possible, and before the start of the final lap went ahead. This tremendous effort seemed to nullify the pain in my foot. Zimny did not really answer my challenge, and I won fairly easily in 8 min. 44 sec. That evening I was due to run a mile at Watford, but my foot was now one raw blister. However, I went to Watford to apologize to the fans for not being able to take part.

The next day I took Madeleine and Christine to Finland for a holiday. I had also been given permission to run and was due to compete in a mile at Naantali on the Wednesday. One of the first things I did in Finland was to visit a chemist's shop to get something for my foot.

Naantali is a beautiful seaside resort, with a population of just over a thousand. Even so, they had their own running-track, built by

A word of thanks to the crowd at the White City

So lonely on the track—leading by a distance in the 1957 A.A.A. Championship three miles. Ibbotson set up a new British record of 13 min. 20·8 sec.

public subscriptions. A Finnish friend of mine had lent me his flat, and it was a pleasant spot for a few days' rest. I tried to forget all about running, and we went yachting and swimming.

Athletics is one of the premier sports in Finland, and the mile race in which I was competing at Naantali caused a tremendous amount of interest. I understand that some spectators travelled up to 600 miles throughout the night to see the race. There was a crowd of more than 10,000 people, and I was surprised to find that there were only two runners apart from myself. The one I had to worry about was Olavi Vuorisalo, the Finnish champion, because the other, Pertil Eraekare, was in the race only as a pace-maker. Vuorisalo was keen to break four minutes, because a Finnish-American had promised a gold watch for the first Finnish runner to achieve this.

The pace-maker went off at a terrific speed, and we were forced to follow. After an opening lap of 56 seconds and a half-mile in 1 min. 56 sec., he dropped out. As I had been in second position the lead was mine. I was in no mood for a fast race, but did want to help Olavi to win that gold watch. He never attempted to take the lead, and at the bell I let everything go. On the home-straight he tried to overtake, but I still had enough left to accelerate again, and finish four yards in front in a time of 3 min. 58·7 sec. He got his gold watch —his time was 3 min. 59·1 sec.

The following day I went to Oslo where I ran in a 5,000-metre event against an international field. Fortunately there were no outstanding rivals and I won, feeling very tired, in 14 min. 13 sec.

My travelling had not finished. The next day I returned to Finland, and three days later found myself running against the three fastest-ever Finnish middle-distance runners, all with the same Christian name of Olavi—Salsola, Vuorisalo and Salonen.

Once again there was a pace-maker—our old friend Eraekare. He seemed to spend all his time running to help others and never having a chance himself. There was a strong wind, but this did not stop Eraekare setting his usual fast pace. When he dropped out I was again in the lead but this time could not find enough speed to counter the finish of Salsola, who won in 4 min 0·2 sec. I was second in 4 min. 0·5 sec.

Really I was amazed that without serious training I could still run such times. Even now I find it difficult to believe. The fact that I had worked so hard during the past winter did not seem the complete answer.

Somehow I had found a mental and physical rhythm that made every demand so easy.

15

Sportsman of the year

I vote for my fellow athlete Derek Ibbotson. Even forgetting his many great performances on the track I think his bubbling sense of fun, good humour and determination make him stand out as a personality.—*June Paul, international athlete*

AFTER Finland there was still no relaxation. On arrival at London Airport Madeleine, Christine and I dashed across London to catch a train at Paddington for Paignton where the following day I was due to run a three miles. This was my fifth competitive race within ten days after more than 2,000 miles of travelling. And, funnily enough, I was enjoying every moment of it. The West Country spectators were magnificent and the race, a handicap, was really tough. I was a back-marker, and one runner received 550 yards start. Coming from the North, I was experienced in handicap races and able to judge my effort so that I won over the last twenty yards in under fourteen minutes. This was just what the spectators wanted, but I had to give everything I had got.

After the Paignton event we had a few days' holiday before going up to Dunoon, Scotland, where I ran a two miles. One of my rivals was Graham Everett, who had beaten me in a heat of the A.A.A. mile championship earlier in the year, and so prevented me from qualifying for the final. Two miles was obviously not his distance. After setting a fast early pace, he lagged badly behind, but this was not the end of the race as Ian Binnie, Scotland's leading distance runner, stayed with me until the last lap. Binnie lacked a finishing 'kick', and I then streaked ahead to a sixty-yard victory in a Scottish All-Comers' record of 8 min. 50·8 sec.

My next major engagement was a 5,000 metres against Russia

at the White City, London. Gordon Pirie was my partner in this race, and we were both disappointed that Vladimir Kuts was not fit enough to compete. Our main rival was a new Russian star Pyotr Bolotnikov. Gordon and I agreed that victory was more important than fast times, and allowed Bolotnikov to make the pace. This he did without being able to emulate Kuts's ability to sprint during alternate laps. The pace was even, allowing Gordon and I to feel comparatively fresh at the last lap. About 300 yards from the tape, I decided to test Bolotnikov, and found he had little resistance. Gordon also had no difficulty in overtaking him, and won the duel with me for first place. So Britain gained major points from this race, although the match proved in favour of Russia. Pirie's time was 13 min. 58·6 sec., and mine 14 min. 0·4 sec.

After a few minor races, I joined the British team for a European tour, which included internationals against Poland in Warsaw and West Germany at Hanover. As usual on such trips, we travelled by chartered aircraft. In Copenhagen Gordon Pirie, who had been competing in Sweden, and his wife, Shirley, joined the team. Some members of the team, especially those who were married, wondered why Mrs. Pirie—formerly Shirley Hampton, an international sprinter—was allowed to accompany him on this trip, while other wives had to stay at home. Shirley and I were old friends. In fact, we had been out together a couple of times—she was still Miss Hampton then—when we were members of the British team which competed against France in Bordeaux in 1955. But I thought our officials were asking for trouble to grant this privilege to one athlete's wife only.

We arrived in Warsaw on Friday evening, and as the match started the following day it gave us little time to settle down. Great prestige is attached to these matches on the Continent, so it would be far better to give a British team a few days' complete rest before the events.

For the first time my ability as a miler was recognized by the national selectors, and I ran in the 1,500 metres. Although I won, it was disappointing that Alan Gordon was just beaten for second place by Stefan Lewandowski, for it meant the loss of valuable points. My time of 3 min. 43·8 sec. was worth a 4 min. 2 sec. mile which pleased me, particularly as I had dallied over the last lap to try and help Alan.

Pirie ran a magnificent race in the 5,000 metres, which he won

Comeback bid. Ibbotson beats John Winch in 4 min. 6·2 sec. at Chiswick to begin his fight back to the top in 1959

Another world record in the making. Ibbotson hands over to Brian Hewson in setting up a world record for the 4 × 1 mile at the White City in 1958. The time was 16 min. 30·8 sec., and the two other legs were run by Peter Clark and Mike Blagrove

Left: Winning a two-mile race at Glasgow Rangers sports

Below: Thundering past Poland's Kazimiers Zimny in a two-mile race at the White City in 1957. Ibbotson won with a three-inch blister on his right foot

with consummate ease while George Knight put up a glittering performance, to run away from the field in the 10,000 metres. Maybe the best individual performance went to that genial giant, Mike Ellis, with a superb series of hammer-throws. The way Continental spectators cheer good field-event performances is an object lesson to British spectators. Unfortunately, Britain lost this match by ten points.

Most of the team stayed on in Poland, but I joined a small party which went on to Helsinki for a mid-week match. On the way we stayed the night in Copenhagen, and it was there that I had a row with Gordon Pirie, of all people.

I was late coming down to join the others for an outing, and Pirie greeted me, 'It's about time you stopped making others wait.'

'You have a lot of room to talk,' I retorted.

The row became more heated, and if officials Harold Abrahams and Clive Adams had not intervened it might have led to blows.

In Helsinki I was due to run a mile, and my rivals were the famous Finnish middle-distance trio, Olavi Vuorisalo, Olavi Salonen and Olavi Salsola. Apparently, the Finns are not very inventive where Christian names are concerned. I had met the three of them on my last trip to Finland, and was just beaten by Salsola, after being forced to lead when the pace-maker dropped out. This time I was prepared for these tactics.

The meeting took place at the Olympic Stadium, and there was a large crowd, including a contingent of British sailors who were in the city to support a British trade fair. The usual pace-maker was in attendance, but this time I made sure I did not take second place behind him. I allowed Salonen this honour, and took over third position.

After the pace-maker cracked, Salonen was left in the lead, and I decided to wait until the last bend before making my effort. Just as I was preparing for the attack I heard an official on the inside of the track shout some sort of command. Immediately Salsola came up to my side. This forced me to change my plans, and I decided to wait until he had passed before sprinting. Salsola continued to run at my shoulder, and then accidentally pushed me, at the same spot in the stadium where Chris Chataway had fallen in the 1952 Olympic Games. I managed to keep my balance but was badly spiked and shaken.

H

While I was trapped by Salsola, the race was being won. Vuorisalo broke on the outside, and Salonen was able to move away in front. When free from the impediment of Salsola, I tried in vain to get back into the race. But it was too late as the two other Finns had captured a long lead. I felt mad, especially as I had disappointed the British sailors. After telling them what had happened, I promised 'I'll have a go at the 3,000 metres.' This was a rash decision as I was in no condition for such a race with only a thirty-five minutes' interval.

I succeeded in staying up with the field, and with 250 yards left was actually in the lead. But when the pressure was on, I discovered all my reserves had been drained out of me by the mile. After this experience in Helsinki, I realized why Finland had been so dominant in middle- and distance-running before the war. They were certainly experts in team tactics, dubious though some of these might appear to be.

There was no time to get my revenge, because the next day we flew on to Germany to join the main British party in a sports camp just outside Hanover. I do not altogether favour these assembly camps before an international match. Competitors who have been away from home for some time become bored by the secluded life.

The match with Germany proved a humiliation for Britain. I did not help very much, being beaten into third place in the 1,500 metres. The Germans were almost equal to the Finns as team-runners, and I found that I was not allowed to pass when I tried to make my effort down the back-straight. However, if I had been really good enough, I could have gone wide and still won. This season was beginning to take its toll.

The policy of combining internationals against such powerful countries as Poland and Germany on one trip is sheer folly. A wiser course would be to fly over for one match, return home and then make a separate trip for the other. As the host country usually pays all expenses, long tours cannot be justified on the grounds of economy.

All season I had wanted to run a fast two miles, and the opportunity presented itself when a race at this distance was staged at Turku in Finland. Although it meant making the trip before returning home, I was keen to go. Gordon Pirie, John Disley and Olavi Vuorisalo were competing, so I was certain it would be a fast time.

When our dear friend the pace-maker dropped out before the three-quarter-mile mark, I took over the lead. This did not worry me on this occasion as I was primarily intent on a fast time. Over the last fifty yards I was overtaken by Vuorisalo and Pirie. As a consolation I recorded my fastest time ever for the two miles, 8 min. 41·2 sec., for third place.

Back in England the international season continued with matches against Poland in London and Glasgow. My winning streak had spent itself. Ken Wood won the 1,500 metres at the White City, with Stefan Lewandowski second and myself third. In Glasgow I was again beaten by Lewandowski.

The end of the year brought a great honour. The Sports Writers' Association elected me their 'Sportsman of the Year'. I was also elected top of the 'Sportsman of the Year' Poll conducted by the *Daily Express*. The Amateur Athletic Association awarded me the C. N. Jackson Memorial Cup as the outstanding United Kingdom athlete of 1957, and I also received the Harvey Memorial Gold Cup for the best performance in the National Championships.

A touching award was that of the Finnish President, Mr. Urho Kekkonen, who sent a personal gift of silver which was presented to me at the Finnish Embassy in London. Mr. Kekkonen had been present in Naantali when I won a mile in 3 min. 58·7 sec.

There's luck under a seven, as they say, and 1957 was certainly my lucky year. I also wore No. 71 when I ran my world record mile.

16

I finish 251st

Cocky, rash, ambitious, confident. These adjectives have
been cut to fit the wiry, high-cheeked figure of George Derek
Ibbotson. He wears them well in Press interviews.—*Vancouver
Province*

MY LAST few races in 1957 convinced me I was mentally
tired of running. Even the desire to win was almost gone.
In Manchester, October 19th, I had my forty-eighth race of
the season. It was over a mile, and I finished a poor third. I could not
whip up the enthusiasm which had given me two victories in an
evening at Birmingham a fortnight previously. Then my first race was
over two miles, which I won and the prize was valued at six guineas.
Madeleine and I were building up our home, and we wanted some
sheets and blankets which were among the prizes, but they were
valued at eight pounds. It was against my Yorkshire nature to pay
hard cash, if it could be avoided, so I decided to run in the mile
event later in the evening. I knew that if I could finish in the first
three, my prize would be worth the extra couple of pounds needed.
Two hours later I lined up in a field which included Mike Blagrove,
Alan Gordon and Mike Berisford, all internationals.

It seemed Berisford and Gordon had decided to set a fast pace
to kill me off. They realized I must be tired after running the two
miles earlier. And I really did feel the pressure of the first lap in
59 seconds, followed by another in 62 seconds. I was then in third
position, but soon found myself fourth, as Blagrove overtook me
when there were 600 yards to go, while Gordon and Berisford were
well ahead.

I was now afraid I would not even get third, and went off after
Blagrove, managing to pass him at the start of the last lap. My first

116

reaction was to be satisfied with third place. But my competitive spirit was too strong, and I found myself compelled to go after Gordon and Berisford. They had tried to break me at the start, and now I wanted to break them at the finish. It was like being goaded by some unseen adviser back into the battle. When I regained contact, the old magic of running flowed back into my veins. The desire for success drove out tiredness, and I managed to win by a few yards. So Madeleine and I got our prize.

Before the end of October everyone—sports writers, casual acquaintances, and even people in the street—were telling me I must rest. Somehow a complete break from athletics had never appealed to me, and I was not sure whether it would be a wise course.

In 1955 I ran a total of fifty-six races—eight more than 1957—but then nobody bothered to give me advice. Maybe because I was not so well known.

Unfortunately, I listened to the wiseacres, and decided to relax completely. I went to parties, stayed up late, and forgot all about running. For the first time I let myself bask in the phoney spotlight of hero-worship. Regretfully I must confess I enjoyed it. In the past I had always resisted the temptations, now I could give vent to my latent relish for the so-called good things of life. Don't believe those legends about Yorkshiremen always being so dour. The county has produced its quota of gay-dogs, and for a period I added one more to their number.

It might have been different had not the British Board turned down invitations for me to run in either South Africa or Australia during the close season. It was pointed out that I needed a rest, and further running would be harmful to my career next season. The irony of this was soon to be apparent. If I had been allowed to run in Australia, I would have met Herb Elliott on the eve of his great season. What an inspiration this could have been to me.

Tennis players and footballers play all the year round with success. I do not believe there is such a thing as physical staleness. As I have pointed out earlier, it is possible to get mentally fed up with racing, but you soon recover. I had proved this to myself during the 1957 season when I sometimes ran almost every day of the week.

In November, G. L. N. Dunne, Secretary of the English Cross-Country Union, asked me whether I would like to run in the

Criterion Des As, an international cross-country race at Evere, near Brussels. The Belgians had specifically asked for me to compete. On my previous trips to Belgium I had been successful over the country. I also enjoyed the visits because I speak French fairly well. It was only a six-mile race, so I accepted.

It was a tragic mistake. I had trained too little. The course was muddy, including hurdles, and there were representatives from many European countries in the field of twenty-nine. The first mile was easy, and I led comfortably, but at the half-way stage I found myself in the rear, fighting it out with a Frenchman, Roger Anselin. He tripped and fell, and it seemed I would at least avoid complete humiliation. But worse was to come. He recovered and overtook me with a mile left. The large Belgian crowd appeared sympathetic, but surprised to see me trailing a bad last. 'What are you doing, Ibbotson?' they shouted in French.

This was the first time in my career I had finished last in a race— almost two minutes behind Anselin. To make matters worse, the junior race which was to follow had to be held up to prevent me being engulfed by runners. This should have taught me a lesson. At more than eleven stone, I was a stone over-weight.

Unfortunately, I forget too easily, and within a week of this race it all seemed just like a bad dream which would never happen again. My buoyancy returned, and I found glib excuses to account for my failure. After all I was still the world's fastest miler. Little did I appreciate that this was a tragic illusion now. During the winter of 1957-8 for five months I did not train properly. After Christmas, when I decided to get down to hard work, I was badly affected by boils. This held me up for another few weeks, but even then I could not train as was necessary because I carried too much weight.

It was about this time that Madeleine and I moved into our new bungalow which had been called 'Myleta'—after a suggestion in a poll conducted by the *News Chronicle*. Getting the house into ship-shape meant working until late in the evening, and often around mid-night we decided to go for a run. Of course, this did no good. I also made the mistake of training too much with Madeleine. Although she is an international athlete, her tempo of running did not suit me. Often I would have to turn back in the darkness to find her, and so lose my concentration. For the first time in my life I found training onerous. But I decided to enter the Southern Cross-Country Championship, and hoped that competition might lift me out of my lethargy.

The race was held at Parliament Hill Fields, where the year before I had run sixth in the National Championship. This time I finished 197th.

South London Harriers, my club, retained their confidence in my ability, and selected me to compete in the National Cross-Country Championship at Birkenhead Park in March. If I had shown more wisdom, I would have withdrawn from cross-country competition, and concentrated wholeheartedly on training for the track. But I did not even have the sense to have a regular weekly run with my old club, Longwood Harriers, to gauge how I was improving. You can only test yourself by running against opponents or the clock. It is impossible to judge speed in cross-country in the same way as on the track. I was of little help to South London Harriers in the National because I finished 251st.

There was no possibility of me running well until I reduced my racing weight. As I like my food, the pounds came off slowly. In 1957 I had accepted an invitation to run at the opening of the Reg Harris Stadium in Fallowfield, Manchester, on April 7th. By this time I was nowhere near fit enough for the track, but thought the two races, mile and two miles, might be good for training. When I mentioned this, a Manchester sports writer countered with: 'Ibbotson should do his training on the Yorkshire moors, and not expect people to pay hard cash to watch him.' There was a lot of truth in what he said because I finished seventh in both races.

Due to my successes of the previous year, I had received a large number of requests to run all over the country, and accepted many of them. This meant that I began the summer with an intensive programme when I was not in the right physical or mental condition to meet it. It was too late now to make up for the lost months of training, but I hoped competition would draw me out and bring me back to my best. After some early failures, it looked as if my old form was returning, when at Manchester on May 17th I ran a mile in 4 min. 9·8 sec., and three-quarters of an hour later gained my first victory of the season over two miles in 9 min. 8 sec.

Two days later I ran in Dublin and beat Gordon Pirie easily over three miles in a comparatively good time of 14 min. 0·7 sec.

Within twenty-four hours I met Ron Delany and Brian Hewson over the mile, and was beaten into third place by only a few yards. It was encouraging.

The first major athletics meeting in Britain is always the British Games and Inter-Counties Championships at the White City, London, during Whitsun. I had been entered for the mile by Yorkshire. The same time-qualifying system, which had caused my elimination in the A.A.A. 1957 Championships, operated at this meeting. Once again I failed to get into the final. I ran second to Mike Blagrove—the same man who had set the pace in my world record mile—with a time of 4 min. 12·7 sec., and missed being among the five fastest losers by a fifth of a second.

After the race I was talking to newspaper men, and pointing out how the athletes hated this system, when the former British team manager, Jack Crump, passed by. I also gave him my views. He told me not to make excuses. A row broke out, and I told him to ask Brian Hewson, who was among the finalists, what he thought of the 'time-trial'. I was so angry that I said I would never run again in such a race—'and that goes for the A.A.A. Championships as well.' This remark, said in the heat of the moment, was to result in my own downfall.

On the Whit Monday I ran in the international two miles, and although I finished third to the Hungarian, Miklos Szabo, and Pirie, my time of 8 min. 47·6 sec. was very satisfactory. Nevertheless, the fact that I was not winning, as in the previous year, sparked off a lot of criticism. It was suggested in the Press that I should be withdrawn from the trip to Vancouver in June, to make way for Brian Hewson. The British officials did not take heed of this advice, and early in June I left with a small British team, which included George Knight, Mike Farrell and John Wrighton, and with Jack Crump as team manager, for Canada.

As we were flying the Polar route, we went first to Amsterdam, where engine trouble caused us to be delayed a couple of days. This was advantageous because it gave me a much-needed rest in the sunshine, and we were able to train along the hard sands.

In Vancouver I was due to run in the mile against Merv Lincoln, of Australia, the Polish champion Stefan Lewandowski, and another Australian, Alex Henderson, who was studying in the U.S.A. It was a formidable field, with Lincoln as the favourite, for earlier that year he had beaten four minutes. Although I was the fastest miler in the world at the time, I had shown no form that season. To make matters worse, I was ill on arrival with continuous headaches caused by a boil at the back of my neck. Lewandowski and Wrighton, both doctors, helped me.

I did not share the pessimism of the British Press about my chances, and said so in a number of interviews in Vancouver. The race was built up as yet another 'Mile of the Century', and tipped to surpass even the Empire Games mile of 1954 when Roger Bannister beat John Landy, both breaking four minutes. My only interest was winning, and I had no desire to start chasing the clock. But this was to be decided by the other runners, especially Henderson who considered that if he clocked under four minutes he might be chosen for the Australian team for the Empire Games to be held later that year in Cardiff. Such a pace would also be beneficial to Lincoln because he knew, after a training session we had together, that I was not in top condition. I was puffing and panting like someone who had not run for years.

On the Saturday morning of the race I woke up to find it pouring with rain. So I sang, 'Oh, what a beautiful morning,' which disconcerted Lincoln who had prayed for sunny conditions. This was my type of weather as it was likely to sap Lincoln's speed. He was in magnificent condition, and before the rains came had felt capable of breaking my world time.

During the race I made sure that Lincoln did not get too far ahead, for he was the man to watch—four yards was the widest margin. After a fastish opening half-mile, the third lap was slow and that suited me perfectly. Henderson was still in there over the last lap, but faded before the final stretch. At seventy yards out—exactly at the spot where Bannister had overtaken Landy four years previously—I closed in on Lincoln; but he drew away.

For nearly all the remainder of the race it was the same. Every time I reached Lincoln's shoulder he escaped. But over the last ten yards I managed to reach him, hold him and then brush away the tape a fraction of a second ahead. It was almost a photo-finish, but my time was given as 4 min. 5·4 sec., with Lincoln at 4 min. 5·6 sec. A broadcast to Australia originally announced Lincoln had won.

You can imagine how I felt after this race, all my fears and worries had vanished. I decided hard competition had compensated for lack of training, and that I was now fit to prepare for the Empire and European Championships later in the year.

On my return home I concentrated on the three miles because I had earlier declared my intention of not running in the A.A.A. Championships' mile while the time-qualifying heats system operated. My first race was at Wolverhampton on one of the hottest days of the year, when Peter Radford proved he was Britain's greatest-ever sprinter by clocking a new record of 9·6 seconds for the 100 yards.

In the dressing-room before the race Stan Eldon, the Windsor policeman who had been in such splendid form, told me bluntly, 'I think you're finished as a three-miler, Derek, why don't you concentrate on the mile?' He also added that he did not think much of my British three-mile record. Eldon might have been joking, but he certainly riled me that day. I was determined that whatever happened, I was going to beat him that afternoon.

Eldon went off at his usual fierce pace, and I stuck to his shoulder. We had a tremendous battle, and eventually he cracked. I did not win—victory went to Peter Clark—but my time of 13 min. 46 sec. delighted me as did the fact that Eldon finished behind me.

A week later I won the Northern Counties three-mile title easily, and Press opinion changed about my prospects. In fact, there was speculation upon whether it would be a good thing for me to run in both the one mile and three miles at the Empire Games. Naturally, I wanted to compete in both races, but when asked by one selector indicated a slight preference for the three miles.

When the team was announced there were a number of surprises. I was included only in the three miles, Eldon confined to the six miles, and Pirie named for the one mile. Later Pirie filled the vacant place in the England team for the three miles. This was made known before the A.A.A. Championships, and as Eldon, Pirie and I were all entered for the three miles there was a lot of interest in this event.

Eldon was obviously after revenge, and once again went off at a furious pace. He told me beforehand that he was after my record. I had no choice but to go with him, and for five laps I trailed behind, taunted by his bobbing head. Maiyoro, a coloured Kenyan runner, was up with the leaders, moving gracefully—a direct contrast to my style at the time. I never felt at all happy, and before the end of the sixth lap had to allow the leaders to go away. It was little solace to see Pirie also struggling. I wanted to talk to Gordon, but it was difficult enough finding breath to run. The final disgrace came when I had to throw in the towel after two miles. It was a terrible moment walking across the track while the race for my title was still going on. Only a year ago I had won this event without opposition, in a new record time. During that lonely walk I realized that the decline and fall of Derek Ibbotson was complete.

After this failure I thought there was something medically wrong with me, and decided to have a check-up. I never did because I realized that my occasional good performances that season showed that the ability was still there, but it was hampered by the casualness of my winter's training. You can't buy success on the cheap.

It looked like the end. Criticism was heaped on my head. Even in the North they were saying Alan Cocking, a Yorkshire lad, should take my place at Cardiff.

Gordon Pirie and I trained together before the Empire Games in the hope of recapturing our form in time. I also played a lot of golf and tennis with Merv Lincoln, and, again, this did not please the critics. They felt I should be training all the time. This would have been no good. One is mentally incapable of training non-stop every day.

I must admit I did not have much confidence when I lined up for the Empire Games three miles. Twelve months ago it looked as if I might win this title, but a lot had happened since. The day was warm. I would have preferred it colder. My prospects were poor, and I had to stay with the leaders—which I managed to do for the first two miles. But with more than three laps left, Murray Halberg, the New Zealander who had overcome the handicap of running with a withered arm, began an amazing sprint which broke up the whole field and gave him the title.

The whole tempo of the race changed dramatically, and I did not have the stamina to respond. Once again I was being mocked for not training hard enough during the winter. I deserved it. I had learnt the hard way.

17

Dropped by Britain

Ibbotson burned out? Ibbotson stale? Ibbotson's shot
his bolt? Don't make me laugh.—*Alan Hoby, Sunday Express*

DURING the Empire Games at Cardiff, I formed firm friendships with Herb Elliott, Merv Lincoln and Mike Agostini,
the Trinidad sprinter who represented Canada. Afterwards
they all came home with me. On the way to Huddersfield we stopped
at a pub for a meal and a drink, and Herb was surprised to be congratulated on his running at Cardiff. He did not expect to be recognized. 'I could walk down the main streets of Melbourne and nobody
would say hello,' he said. 'Yet here, out in the sticks, a guy comes up
and shakes my hand. I don't get it.' I doubt whether Herb could now
walk down any street in Australia without being hailed. But then
it was before he shattered the athletics world with his superlative
running in 1958.

It was a hard drive to Huddersfield, made worse by pouring rain
and the pitch-black night. It was nearly midnight before we got home,
and somehow all my guests found somewhere to sleep.

The next day we were all due to run at a meeting at Berwick-on-
Tweed. Madeleine cooked us a big breakfast of cornflakes, bananas,
orange juice, mixed grill with steak, marmalade and toast, coffee
and a few pints of milk. Incidentally food bills during the few days
my pals stayed with us came to £20—such lean and hungry men.

Herb drove my car up to Berwick and just outside Newcastle we
were stopped for speeding. Again he was recognized.

The policeman told him, 'Do you mind slowing down, Mr.
Elliott, we know you're a pretty fast lad on the track, but you're in
the wrong area for speeding at the moment.'

He then escorted us part of the way to Berwick. On arrival we

124

found the meeting had been rained off as it had poured all the previous evening and the track was flooded. So we all trained together with Agostini giving us some idea of a sprinter's speed over a quarter-mile.

After dinner that evening there was a dance, and Herb got merry. He was given a bottle of vodka, and in traditional Australian style didn't bother about a glass. He believed it was a good thing occasionally to break completely from training, and liquor helped him to relax. During our holiday together he drank and smoked quite a lot, but before we left for London he declared, 'I'll not touch another drink or smoke another cigarette until after my next five or six races.'

Less than a week later, in Dublin, he broke my world record with a time of 3 min. 54.5 sec.—there must have been a kick in that vodka!

Herb, Merv and Mike were all keen on helping me get into the team for the European Games in Stockholm, and we trained together at Huddersfield on the winding mill path I used for a track. It came as a surprise to them that I had such poor training facilities. Lincoln acted as 'Big Brother' and would not allow me to stay late at parties.

The following Saturday I ran in the Emsley Carr Mile—the event in which two years previously I had first broken four minutes. There were many talented runners competing in the race, and I felt sure the winner would need an exceptionally fast time.

And I had to prove myself worthy of selection for the 1,500 metres at Stockholm. After the Empire Games I became convinced there was no time to get fit for the 5,000 metres, but believed I had still the ability to set a fast time over 1,500 metres. Unfortunately, the mile at the White City turned out to be a tactical race.

Just as I was about to make my bid for victory, Lincoln cut across, blocking my path. At the same time Murray Halberg came up on the outside, forcing me to check my sprint. There was no time to recover and I was beaten into third place, with a time of 4 min. 7 sec. Although I had beaten Alan Gordon and Graham Everett, both contenders for a European Games place, two of my other rivals, Mike Blagrove and Mike Berisford, had not competed. They were due to run on Monday in the match mile against the Commonwealth. I was assuming the selectors would not consider Brian

Hewson as he had publicly expressed a preference to run in the 800 metres at Stockholm.

On the Sunday I played golf with Elliott, and we discussed my chances of making the British team. Unofficially I had been told that I would be selected, but still felt a little uncertain. Herb suggested I should ask to run in the mile with Blagrove and Berisford to help the selectors decide who was the best.

Times should not be the only guiding factor in athletics selection. They can often be misleading. When a mile is won in a fast time it helps all the competitors to clock their best times. That is why four minutes has been beaten four and five times in one race.

I was due to run in the two miles on the Monday, but realized this would not be helpful to my training for the shorter event, and that a poor performance might jeopardize my prospects of going to Stockholm. It was impossible to contact the British team manager, Les Truelove, before the meeting began, and so I decided to run only in a mile race at Watford on the Monday evening. I would try to improve on the times of Blagrove and Berisford at the White City that afternoon. With this plan in mind, I went to the White City to enjoy the meeting as a spectator, and had a lunch of soup, plaice, chips, fruit salad and coffee. I had just settled myself into a seat, when a tannoy message asked me to report to Les Truelove in the centre of the ground. It was then about 45 minutes before the two-mile race was due to start.

Here is the dialogue that followed:

Truelove: 'Why are you not running in the two miles?'

Ibbotson: 'I don't feel like competing over that distance. I want to be chosen for the 1,500 metres at Stockholm, and don't think a two-mile race will enhance my prospects. It would be better if I concentrated on the mile, and I intend to run at Watford tonight and aim for a faster time than the British runners in the international mile, for which I have not been chosen.'

Truelove: 'That's beside the point. You've accepted to run in the two miles and as far as we are concerned that is what you'll run.'

Ibbotson: 'What difference does it make? I am not running in a team, and I am sure no one will worry if I am missing.'

Truelove: 'I have been instructed, with the full authority of the Board, that if you do not run here this afternoon and instead go to

Watford, there is a good chance that you won't be in the team for Stockholm.'

Ibbotson: 'Then let me run in the international mile.'

Truelove: 'Sorry, you can't do that. We have a full number, and do not want to increase the field. You must think of the crowd.'

Ibbotson: 'I have never let the public down. Last year I ran after an injection for a two-inch blister on my foot. You know this. And I have just had lunch, and would make a right fool of myself if I went out there and ran now. It's only thirty minutes before the start, and I could not possibly be ready.'

Truelove: 'That's beside the point. All I have to say is you are down to run the two miles.'

Ibbotson: 'You are inviting me to destroy my chances of going to Stockholm.'

Truelove: 'We'll have to see about that.'[1]

I was furious at being treated almost like a professional. But what could I do? I ran all the way to the car-park to get my kit, and on entering the dressing-room, someone said, 'I thought you were not running.'

'Truelove has told me to run,' I said.

I decided the only thing I could do was to lead until I got tired. After a mile in 4 min. 20 sec., I had virtually to give up and was easily overtaken. The lunch was rumbling in my stomach and I just could not fight back. So I decided to save some energy for the evening. When I got to Watford, I discovered the two miles had taken its toll of my energy, and the difference with Truelove had upset me.

There was not much opposition in this race, so I cruised round gently for the first three laps and ran the final quarter in 57 seconds. But my time was only 4 min. 17 sec. compared to Blagrove's 4 min. 3·1 sec. and Berisford's 4 min. 3·5 sec.

It still came as a shock when I was not included in the British team for the European Championships, especially as I was given this news by Sydney Hulls, of the *Daily Express*. Apparently, the team list

---

[1] Mr. Leslie Truelove points out the rulings regarding the entering of competitions apply just as much to Ibbotson as anyone else. He states that Ibbotson was advised that for his own good he should observe them. Mr. Truelove also claims his recollection of the conversation at the White City is at very considerable variance with the one given by Derek Ibbotson.

had been sent in advance to Sweden, and it was released from there before the British Board made their announcement.

Brian Hewson and Mike Blagrove were chosen for the 1,500 metres. This meant the selectors had ignored Brian's request to run in the 800 metres. As it turned out, the selectors were proved right this time, because Hewson won the 1,500 metres magnificently. Blagrove was a good lad, but I believed my greater experience should have given me his place.

It was a bitter blow to me. I had arranged my holiday to coincide with the Championships and saved enough money for my wife's fare. I was determined to go, even if only as a spectator.

Everyone was kind. Two newspapers offered to send me to write comments. But the A.A.A. would not give me permission even if I received only my expenses. Why some athletes are allowed to write and others forbidden, is one of those annoying mysteries about athletics.

Eventually I went over with Dr. G. Newbury Box and his wife, from Leatherhead. They were athletics enthusiasts, and only too happy to help Madeleine and myself.

While I was in Stockholm, the Swedish Athletic Federation invited me to live in their camp with some members of the Australian team. It was here that I began training with Herb Elliott and to re-build my career, which had now hit rock-bottom.

While in Sweden I ran a few races including the one in which Elliott broke the world 1,500-metre record with 3 min. 36 sec. This event proved all too dismally that my lack of winter training had left me bereft of the stamina for those vital finishing spurts. I had to admit that despite the effects of circumstances and erroneous advice, I myself had to bear the brunt of the blame. No doubt many times that season I had run away from myself and my own basic convictions.

18

I adopt a Russian formula

Breakfast with Ibbotson is a stimulating affair. His bouncy,
laughing personality wipes away any lurking cobwebs before
the cornflakes are milked. It is no passing cheer.—*John Ross,
Daily Mail*

A T THE height of my success in 1957, I was often asked
'What's the secret, Derek?' as though there were some
mysterious drug or athletics yoga.

But there's only one way to the top in running—blood, sweat
and sometimes tears. Whatever success I enjoyed during the summer
of 1957 can be traced back to the early months of that year when I
trained harder than at any period in my life. I made a resolution to
do this on January 1st, and began work that day only a couple of
weeks after returning from Melbourne.

During the early part of January 1957 I lived at Mitcham,
Surrey, and could train at Tooting Bec track—in fact I even ran to the
track. Often I would return home, after training for more than two
hours, in a state of complete exhaustion—almost unable to undress
myself to bath.

This is not harmful for those who are fit. In athletics you can only
take out what you put in. I wanted to be sure I had plenty in reserve
during the summer. Hard work is the only real secret. And if you want
to know just how hard—look at the training schedules in the appendix of this book. One thing I avoid is training always with the same
people, because of the tendency to run each other into the ground.
This can be harmful psychologically to the one on the losing end.

If you are beaten easily in training, it is difficult to imagine that
the scales will change in competition.

The originator of the formula which brought me the world mile record was a Russian—Vladimir Kuts. During the winter of 1956-7, when I was training one lunch-time with Gordon Pirie and Brian Hewson at Chelsea, we began a discussion on schedules. Pirie said he was going to try the Kuts method of reducing the interval between each set run. I had read about this type of training, and decided to experiment myself.

At the time I considered myself a three-miler—although I had broken four minutes for the mile in 1956. My ambition was to become the leading 5,000-metre runner in the world and avenge the defeat I suffered from Kuts in the Olympic Games. What could be better than to use his own ideas? It was no easy task reducing the interval of rest between each training run, and after much gruelling application I managed to get down to 45 seconds compared to my usual 90 seconds.

Most people, including coaches, thought I was mad, but the results proved I was on the right lines. And, I became the fastest miler in the world by using the ideas of a distance runner. There is no universal formula which suits everyone. That is the fascination about running.

For example, Brian Hewson, the 1958 European 1,500-metre champion, never attempted such a short recovery rate. When we trained together he would usually run two quarter-miles to my three, but a little faster. He was a better half-miler, and relied more on speed than stamina. It is doubtful whether he would have benefited from the Kuts technique.

It is doubtful whether a coach would have approved of my experiment. But as I have never had a coach, I am more prepared to try something which appeals to me.

Most people, especially foreigners, are amazed to discover I am virtually self-taught. This is not because I disapprove of coaches. In fact I believe that Britain could do with more of them. Our top coaches are equal to any in the world, but none of the professionals are able to concentrate solely on teaching athletes.

The coach must be on the spot to conduct training, adjust technical faults and use his persuasion to get extra work. In the North it is very difficult to find this advice, which could be so vital in the early years of an athlete's career. Leading runners who have been coached are later able to work on their own because they have been put on the right lines.

Before a major race, it can be stimulating to talk to someone who knows your ability and that of the opposition. Franz Stampfl helped Bannister and Chataway a great deal to prepare mentally for the big occasion. On the other hand, Herb Elliott once refused to discuss tactics with his coach, Percy Cerutty. This was before the Empire Games half-mile in 1958 when Elliott was due to meet Brian Hewson and Mike Rawson, who had defeated him over this distance at the A.A.A. Championships. Cerutty suggested discussing the race. Elliott replied that if he did not know how to run then he never would. Elliott used entirely different tactics from those he tried in the A.A.A. Championships. This time he waited until the half-way stage before going into the lead, and won comfortably against Brian Hewson, much to the surprise of the experts.

I received valuable assistance during my career mainly from Cyril Foster, of Longwood Harriers, Squadron-Leader D. C. Davis in the R.A.F. and Franz Stampfl, who provided me with training schedules when I first came into prominence. All helped more as advisors than coaches.

When I was in Budapest I met Mighali Igloi, who was the brains behind the great Hungarian middle-distance runners. Before escaping to the U.S.A. after the revolution, he coached Sandor Iharos, Istvan Roszavolgi and Laszlo Tabori.

There is an international brotherhood among the leading coaches, and they are nearly all prepared to help athletes with their ideas. That is why Igloi took the trouble to advise me, even though it could prove a danger to his own interests. He said I wasted an immense amount of effort in my running by not using the correct stride and keeping my arms too high. I was impressed by the way he ran his training sessions.

When Roszavolgi, Iharos and Tabori met Igloi for training, they had no idea what they were expected to do. Igloi considered it might have a bad effect if they were allowed to brood on the prospect of running forty 440 yards in one session. So they would start, never knowing when they were due to finish, and consequently put in a 100 per cent effort all the time. Igloi could sense by the way his pupils were running whether he could increase the work.

He has not had the same success in the U.S.A., perhaps due to language difficulties or because he is dealing with a different temperamental set-up.

My training approach is similar to Igloi's. I often go to the track intending to begin with ten quarters in 60 seconds each, with only short recovery intervals. After this I decide what to do next. More often than not, I will join other athletes and follow their schedules. By this method, or lack of method, I work harder than my rivals.

Franz Stampfl built up his reputation when in London conducting a free-lance athletics school. Among the many fine athletes he has advised are Roger Bannister, Chris Chataway, Brian Hewson, Chris Brasher and Merv Lincoln.

Stampfl believes in pre-planned schedules, and when he went to Australia in 1956 he tape-recorded talks to his pupils. This was the ideal method for Stampfl, who is essentially a 'personality coach'. He knows how to get the best out of individuals.

When I ran against Lincoln and Hewson in the mile at Los Angeles in 1957, Stampfl, I believe, regarded me as the main threat to his men, but told me disparagingly, 'You should stick to the three miles—that's your distance, Derek.'

Then he jokingly jibed at me with some comment about Yorkshiremen being 'uncivilized'. This niggled me into an 'I'll show Stampfl and his boys' mood. Foolishly, I decided to set the pace. The result: 1. Lincoln, 2. Hewson, 3. Tabori, 4. Ibbotson. And that complacent smile remained on Stampfl's face.

Another coach of international fame is Percy Cerutty, and his ideas are completely opposed to those of Stampfl. Among the many brilliant runners Cerutty has coached are John Landy and Herb Elliott. He has taught them to ignore training schedules and stop-watches, and run by instinct . . . over the sand-dunes at Portsea, Victoria, where he lives.

Cerutty's uncanny beneficial influence over athletes cannot be disputed. I wanted to accept his generous offer to live and train at Portsea during the winter of 1958-9, but it was not possible owing to family ties and financial difficulties.

The chief British coach, Geoff Dyson, excels in the scientific side of track and field, but does not have enough time to spend on individuals. As part of his salary is paid by the Ministry of Education, he is forced to travel around the country teaching voluntary coaches. It would be better if the British athletic authorities could find the money to pay his full salary so that he could concentrate on the improvement of British athletes.

Nevertheless, he has enjoyed success with such men as shot-putters John Savidge, Arthur Rowe, steeplechaser John Disley and pole-vaulter Geoff Elliott.

As Britain's professionals are all involved mainly in lecturing to the amateur coaches, men like Squadron-Leader D. C. Davis take over the important role of helping youngsters to improve. They get little of the glory, but without them Britain would not be a major athletic power. Fortunately they find that objective sufficient reward in itself.

19

Sex in sport

There are so many young ladies with gorgeous figures and handsome young men with athletic torsos assembled here that the Olympic fun and games are no longer confined to the racing-tracks.—*Maurice Smith, The People*

WHEN the article from which this quotation is taken appeared just before the start of the 1956 Olympic Games it caused a hell of a flap in high quarters. Had international amity in the Olympic Village passed the platonic stage? Quite likely there was a bit of slap and tickle, but as most of the competitors had devoted a large part of their lives to reaching Olympic standards they were not likely to jeopardize their prospects.

But I think it is time the truth was told about the sex lives of athletes, because so much that is inaccurate has been hinted at. Wherever you have large groups of healthy young people thrown together in an exciting nerve-testing atmosphere, there is bound to be a certain amount of necking. Sometimes these friendships turn to real love. Not even the nine-foot wire fence or Army guard round the women's quarters can stop this. Love, as they say, will find a way.

In fact at Melbourne one romance overcame even the political Iron Curtain. American Olympic hammer-throwing champion Harold Connolly met the beautiful Olga Fikotova from Czechoslovakia, in the Olympic Village.

Their love, no doubt, helped to inspire both of them to win Olympic gold medals. They wanted to marry in Australia, but the long arm of Communism had stretched across the world.

So Olga returned to Prague and Harold to Boston.

But this love affair, which surely is the modern counterpart to the legendary romances of the ages of chivalry, could not be extinguished.

In 1957 Connolly toured Europe as a hammer-thrower and visited Prague. There he pleaded with the President of Czechoslovakia for permission to marry his lovely Olga. Such ardour in the end even thawed the dialectical materialists, and the two Olympic champions from different worlds were married in Prague with Emil Zatopek best man, and Dana Zatopekova the maid of honour.

Who says sport does more harm than good in international relationships?

Not all the couples you see holding hands in Olympic camps are on the threshold of marriage, but usually their friendships are quite wholesome.

At the same time I do not want to give the impression that sex presents no problems. It is commonplace that a high degree of fitness tends to promote rather than diminish one's physical desires. An athlete is more tempted to sexual indulgence than, say, an office-worker. But to counteract this an athlete, to reach the top, must severely discipline himself.

The same applies to women athletes. Training and rest must take priority over parties and drinking. Thus will-power and character are strengthened. The desire to succeed provides the power to resist many temptations.

Dressing-room small talk has it that a few athletes thrive on sex. They are the we-live-only-once types who draw on their natural reserves until they are exhausted. I don't believe the Don Juans can last very long in top-class athletics.

The ideal is for an international athlete to be married to an athlete as they both understand each other's problems and can arrange their lives accordingly. At the same time I do not think married couples should share the same room when on tours. This is not permissible in such events as the Olympic or Empire Games, where the women have separate quarters.

In my experience I have found that lack of control is more often found among sportswomen. There have been some extreme cases. One well-known Dutch sprinter was warned she would be banned from further international matches abroad unless she stopped associating with various men in other teams.

There was similar trouble in the Hungarian camp. I once asked what had happened to a well-known Hungarian distance-runner, who looked like developing into world-class.

A Hungarian athlete shrugged his shoulders and said: 'He fell in the clutches of . . .' mentioning the name of a universally known and brilliant woman athlete.

Then, there are the camp-followers—women who are attracted to well-known athletes and attend the various meetings. Then after the race they arrange an introduction and invite their particular favourite home for coffee—with breakfast to follow if desired! This often happens in Scandinavian countries.

When I was in Stockholm during the European Championships I was told of the troubles experienced by World Cup football teams. The Mexicans moved from the first to the fifth floor of their hotel to stop the 'blonde tigresses' invading their rooms. One team threatened to leave Stockholm and live on a boat in the harbour.

Villages full of sportsmen always attract the professional good-time girls. At Melbourne the police had a clear out and found scores of prostitutes among the visitors to the camp. At the Empire Games in Cardiff in 1958, a check was made, after complaints, on girls who attended dances. This screening was not very effective as many lads were still invited to take 'a walk in the fields'.

But this is not uniquely a sporting problem. This type of woman will always be attracted to camps, as any Serviceman can confirm, and men who associate with them would do so anyway without living in an Olympic Village.

Many athletes severely curb their marital relationships lest it takes the edge off their fitness. In my view it has little effect on the physically fit because their powers of recovery are greater. At the same time there should be at least two days' abstention before a major race. This might make a difference of half a second over a mile. (Don't ask me how I calculate it!)

Married life should be as normal as possible to avoid frustration and nerves. The ability to mentally and physically relax is one of the important keys to sporting success.

And I have no time for some of the weird forms of duress applied to bachelors, the oddest of which was the custom of one coach who tied cotton reels to his trainees' pyjamas to prevent them sleeping on their backs, in order to reduce the range of their sub-conscious imaginations.

Coloured runners seem better blessed. They appear less affected by parties and gay evenings. I have known men who could stay out until dawn and still produce world-class performances on the track the next evening.

This might be explained by the fact that most coloured athletes excel at the shorter distances. I doubt whether they could continue a hectic social life if they ran events from the mile upwards.

The fear that the physical side of marriage can upset athletic performances has caused divorces in Finland. Dennis Johansson, a Finnish national coach and former Olympic runner, told me of athletes who refused to associate with their wives during the three-month training build-up prior to a season. 'There was one chap who lived an abnormal married life for ten months of the year and his wife divorced him,' Johansson said.

'Finnish women do not compete in sports in the same way as women in other countries. Therefore it is more difficult for them to help their husbands blend marriage and sport.'

We have all heard those whispered explanations of an athlete's decline: 'That's what marriage does for you, old chap.' There is some truth in this, but I think the effect is caused more by the tendency to take life easier and over-eating than sexual indulgence.

When your wife encourages you to put your feet up in front of the fire and watch TV it is tempting to miss a training session, especially in bad weather. Life becomes too easy.

For the last word I hand over to my wife Madeleine—she says:

'At least men are not upset by menstruation. Some of our finest girl internationals are seriously affected. When I was seventeen I was not right for seven months and the doctor told me it was due to the physical shock of running when not in a fit condition. Every girl who wants to take up sport should see her doctor.

'On the other hand, it is definitely easier for the athletic woman to have a baby—recovery is quicker and muscle control stronger.'

20

The phoney set-up

I've said before that the whole amateur rule as it stands at present should be scrapped and that we should, instead, set up 'condition of entry' for anyone who wishes to compete under A.A.A. auspices.—*Harold Abrahams, World Sports*

THE 1948 Olympic Games in London started a terrific boost in the popularity of athletics. Many youngsters began to regard it as more exciting than other sports and the general public began taking a much greater interest. The A.A.A. inaugurated an excellent coaching scheme which introduced advanced training techniques to clubs and encouraged schools to give more time to the sport. Television quickly appreciated the importance of running as a spectacle.

Credit must also go to officials, who worked in the background to build up athletics within a few years as a major sport. Few anticipated how rapid the rise would be and so the work, and later the power, was left in too few hands. The consequences of this have been serious, for the growth has outspeeded the modernization of its government.

It is important to understand how athletics in Britain is controlled. The Amateur Athletic Association is the parent body to which clubs in England are affiliated. The Association, run by the clubs, controls the laws which govern the sport. The Association's main source of income is derived from the annual championships, but this is not sufficient these days, due partly to the cost of the coaching scheme.

As the laws of the International Amateur Athletic Federation— the governing authority in world athletics—do not allow countries under one political government to be represented separately, a committee had to be formed before the last war, to act on behalf of England, Wales, Scotland and Northern Ireland. This is called the British Amateur Athletic Board which controls all international matches where the label 'Britain' is used. As this applies to the Olympic Games, European Championships and the majority of matches, it can be seen that this small committee has become all-powerful.

There are many aspects of British athletics administration which can be admired and other countries have used it as a model. But from the point of view of an active athlete I consider many leading officials are too old and out of touch with the aspirations and needs of competitors. That is why I advocate an age limit of fifty-five for men serving on important committees or holding high offices. Some good men might be lost by such a rigid rule, but at least it would ensure an earlier chance for younger, and often more enterprising men.

I have heard it said the sport could not do without Mr. ——. That is often said about competitors. When Roger Bannister retired there were many who considered this would mark the end of Britain's domination of the mile and 1,500 metres. Yet within months, Chris Chataway and Brian Hewson had broken four minutes. In 1958 Hewson went on to retain for Britain the European 1,500-metre crown which Bannister had won in 1954. No one is indispensable—competitor or official.

When Bannister ceased to be an active athlete he was no longer tied by the stringent amateur laws and therefore was able to give television broadcasts and write for newspapers. In other words he was able to exploit athletics for gain, and must now, I imagine, be legally regarded as a professional. The same laws do not seem to apply to officials and this is what causes so much resentment among athletes.

Members of the public cannot understand why administrators can make money out of the sport while it is forbidden to competitors. Nor can I.

The names of Jack Crump and Harold Abrahams are familiar to millions of newspaper readers, radio listeners and television viewers. For more than twenty years Crump was manager of the British team and is still secretary of the British Amateur Athletic Board—that exclusive but powerful committee to which I have referred. Abrahams is honorary treasurer of the same Board. Officially, neither are international selectors, but I personally would have thought that they must have some effect on a number of decisions without actually voting. Both are able speakers in committees.

Abrahams read law when at Cambridge, and also has the right athletic background because he won an Olympic gold medal in the 100 metres in Paris in 1924. From what Abrahams has written it would seem he agrees with me that the amateur laws are outdated. I only hope his able brain will help to change them.

Until they are changed I think he should realize the strong feeling among competitors over financial 'perks' appearing to be the exclusive right of officials.

Crump cannot claim the same notable athletic achievements as the man with whom he is often associated, but he is a tremendous worker for the sport and has played a bigger role than anyone to raise it from a Cinderella position in Britain. He is efficient and I can recall few snags when he was team manager. But I maintain that it would be better if he did not act as a leading administrator one moment and a journalist-broadcaster the next. The administration should always be aloof from the cut-and-thrust of Press and broadcasting. This dual role of some officials has brought critical comment by the International Athletes Club.

Before the 1956 Olympic Games at Melbourne, Crump gave his forecasts in *World Sports* of the likely winners and included only two British athletes—Gordon Pirie and Thelma Hopkins. This made me train harder as I lost my temper. Surely it is not for the team manager to make such forecasts? I can assure you it did not help in building the confidence needed at Melbourne.

This was not Crump's first attempt at such forecasting. In the same magazine he forecast winners for the Helsinki Olympic Games in 1952.

My views won't be popular because members of the Board do not appear to welcome criticism. They made that obvious when they refused to accept a letter from Derek Johnson condemning the method of selection and stating that athletes were not 'performing monkeys'. They did not even investigate the letter to judge whether it contained any worth-while points. Their attitude was, 'Who is this Johnson to criticize us?'

Athletes are not the only ones subjected to this high-handed attitude. It also happens to the coaches. When the British team was in Warsaw for the match against Poland in 1957, coach Geoff Dyson threatened to resign because he claimed the relay order was changed without his knowledge. Dyson is one of the most brilliant coaches in the world and he took this stand to establish a fundamental principle which is accepted by all other countries. The attitude of officials seems to be that they only consult the coach if *they* consider it necessary. Britain's international success will increase when coaches are given the power their position deserves.

One reason why Poland has made such a dramatic climb as an athletics nation during recent years is the encouragement their coaches are given. And it is from their ranks that most of the leading administrators are drawn. Our professional coaches should be given charge of small teams on short trips to Europe during the season.

If they had more say in team management, young athletes would receive a more helpful introduction to the international scene. When I represented Britain for the first time, in the match against Germany, I was amazed that the team manager did not even discuss our race beforehand. As it happened, Chataway and myself had agreed to use the race to break the world record, but an expert on tactics would have been able to give us many useful hints. At least nowadays we are given times of the main opposition in the international matches. More information of this type would be helpful.

A broader vision is needed in British athletics if the sport is to continue its amazing growth. New men must be brought in. Room at the top must be found for international athletes with the right qualifications, so that they can make valuable contributions from their recent knowledge of combat on the track or field. If they are left to meander along the normal sluggish path their freshness will be lost and they will be out of date themselves when their turn to take over at long last arrives.

Now I would like to discuss an even more controversial subject —do amateur athletes get paid for running? Of course, some of them do! This is known to leading officials, but they do not take action as it cannot be proved. Suspicions and rumours do not constitute evidence and I have no intention of sparking off a witch-hunt.

Every international athlete has heard stories about illegal payments and many have been offered liberal expenses or lump sums to run at certain meetings. But this is not as common as is generally believed. When these approaches have been made to me I have always refused because my amateur status is too important to sacrifice for a few pounds. I get tremendous pleasure out of actual competition. These conversations always take place without any witnesses and, if alleged, would certainly be denied by those who make the offer.

There seems to me nothing wrong for a competitor to be allowed to make money out of athletics. When the amateur laws were originally framed they referred to members of the gentry who could afford to indulge in sport and forget work. Now we have the paradox of State-aided athletes in Communist countries whose sporting activities are regarded as work. As they are not officially paid for performing in sport they can remain amateurs and take the high and mighty Olympic oaths without disturbing their consciences too much. A Communist sporting star lives a better life than most of his countrymen. He has smarter clothes (often bought in the West), a good flat and sometimes even a car—a real luxury.

But it would be wrong to give the impression that all the evasions of amateur rules are to be found behind the Iron Curtain. The Americans have their own system of fostering their stars through the athletics scholarship, under which sportsmen receive allowances for almost nominal jobs. I like best the story of the athlete who was paid for winding the gymnasium clock. It appears that a four-minute miler makes a more efficient winder-upper-of-clocks than one who can manage only 4 min. 5 sec. So the pay of the four-minute man is, say, £15 a week, and the scale declines according to the drop in athletic ability.

Also Australia reached world supremacy at swimming by keeping their best competitors together in camps for a long period before the 1956 Olympic Games.

I have heard it said in Scandinavia that it is sometimes cheaper to bring over a foreign athlete than to get one of their own runners for a meeting. There are many stories of how competitors make running worth while. Some suggest that professional running is not feasible in Europe because the 'amateurs' are doing too well to make the switch.

But I would like to see all the hypocrisy swept aside and an honest introduction of full-blooded professionalism.

Fees would obviously depend on the box-office value of the performer. If I had been paid according to my worth during the 1957 season, I could have given my married life a terrific send-off. As it was I sometimes had difficulty getting legitimate expenses. Imagine the money I might have made out of television, broadcasting, newspapers and advertising. Would it in any way have been reprehensible? Did anyone regard Denis Compton or Johnny Haynes as unethical? Of course not. After I broke the world mile record I was thirsty and found a bottle of milk on the competitors' bench. As I took a swig, photographers, who were following me like hawks, snapped me. When the photograph appeared there was a suggestion from certain members of the National Farmers' Union that they should get an active sportsman to advertise their milk as well as the pretty Miss Zoë Newton.

If this had been possible, it would have provided me with a useful income. At least, like most sportsmen, I *do* drink milk. But the amateur laws prevented me making money in this way. The ironical twist to this incident is that Jack Crump, when British team manager, did advertise milk, as he was perfectly entitled to as an official and not an athlete.

No, the amateur laws are crazy and full of anomalies. They are repeatedly broken and nothing is done about these transgressions. So why not reframe them—if complete professionalism is still considered taboo. Even if the athlete were not allowed to be paid for performing, he should be able to receive financial benefits for what the law calls 'exploiting amateur status'. The athlete would still compete in the National Championships without payment because the publicity and status of a title would be vital to him in gaining his extras.

This works well in table tennis, where registered players can be paid for lectures, exhibitions, writing and broadcasting. It is the only answer the West has to combat the Communistic method of finding a loophole in the present laws.

Some people have the notion that officials would not continue their voluntary work if athletes were picking up 'perks'. If this were the case they would have resigned already. And there is no danger of the lesser-known athletes refusing to compete in events in which others are being paid. They would be only too eager to prove themselves worthy of a fee.

But even if professionalism were introduced, I would advise all athletes to give priority to their ordinary jobs. Few can continue successfully on the track after the age of thirty. And being yesterday's hero provides no meal-ticket.

21

Track greats

Derek Ibbotson bamboozled me. The so-and-so beat me with a spot of psychology. He told us all he wasn't fit or ready. Then before I know it there he is in the stretch breathing down my neck. I can't believe it, but there he is. It taught me a lesson. Never listen to an Englishman.—*Merv Lincoln after the mile in Vancouver, 1958*

AFTER reaching prominence in 1955 I had the privilege of running against many of the finest athletes in the world, including three whom I class as all-time greats—Zatopek, Kuts and Elliott. It is a tremendous performance to be a world champion at one distance, but men like Zatopek and Kuts excelled over a range of events. Zatopek's feat of winning the Olympic 5,000 metres, 10,000 metres and marathon in Helsinki in 1952 during one week may never be equalled. Every year competition becomes more severe.

I rank Gordon Pirie the greatest British athlete of my time because his successful range of distances extended from 1,500 to 10,000 metres and the cross-country. More than any other individual he inspired British youth to test themselves in the most gruelling of sports—middle and distance running. Track greats have one thing in common—a high intelligence. Without it they could not survive the cut-and-thrust of international competition. The track is a lonely place and it needs strength of mind and body to survive. And these are the men who had these qualities:

GORDON PIRIE

A fine competitor, never beaten until the tape was broken. Some runners will not come back after they are passed, but Pirie always does.

He fights all the way. As a young man Pirie was carefree, and even mischievous. To attain his goal he had to change his temperament completely. He drove himself remorselessly under fantastic training schedules. I could never undertake such a programme. In fact, I believe Pirie has lost many of his races on the training tracks. In the history of British distance running he has played a vital role and broken five world records. This is a tribute to his remarkable tenacity.

DEREK JOHNSON

He ran second in the 800 metres in Melbourne and was the most talented post-war British athlete in my time. He beat 10 seconds for 100 yards and excelled over races up to a mile, ran a successful 3,000-metre steeplechase and hurdled with the best. Johnson is proof that the brilliant junior can continue his career into senior ranks.

ROGER BANNISTER

I never ran against Bannister, the man I replaced as British mile record-holder. He retired in 1954 before I had come to the fore. Bannister will always have an historic place as the first man to break the four-minute barrier. I have little in common with Bannister except the ability to run a fast mile. His policy of competing in only three or four major races a season was alien to me. It is a good thing few athletes follow this policy, otherwise the sport would die.

CHRIS CHATAWAY

He has repeatedly found his way into this book. This is only to be expected as our careers crossed so many times. I have been critical of his approach to running, but my admiration for him as a man who refused to accept defeat is unstinted. Chataway had tremendous will-power and was a rare personality. He was always an attraction to the crowds.

KEN WOOD

A rival of mine from the early days in Yorkshire when I first took up competitive running. He might have been the world's greatest 5,000-metre runner—better than Pirie or Chataway—if he had been prepared to devote more time to training. After Melbourne he seemed to lose interest—some said his confidence had gone. He had the speed and strength to win the 1956 Olympic 1,500 metres but tactically ran a bad race. If he had moved up to a nearer position and sprinted later I doubt whether even Ron Delany would have held him. What a wasted potential!

BRIAN HEWSON

One of the most delightful stylists who has graced the British tracks, but so often on the big occasions he lacked that 'needle'. He should have been at least in the first three at Melbourne, instead of fifth. He partially compensated for this by winning the European 1,500-metre title. Maybe Hewson should have remained a half-miler. Tom Courtney, the American Olympic 800-metre champion, regarded him as a real threat. Hewson is the gazelle of the track—swift, rhythmic but frail.

STAN ELDON

Physically Eldon was a great athlete, but he was a poor tactician. In 1958 he made a similar mistake in both the Empire Games and European Championships by leading most of the way. This was madness in view of Eldon's finishing speed. Before the Stockholm races I suggested he should not try to break away from the field until after mid-way—and later if possible. But he became over-eager and broke away too early. Before the end Krzyszkowiak caught him and Eldon could not answer the final sprint. Eldon modelled his style too closely on that of Kuts. But different men need different styles.

VLADIMIR KUTS

A man apart. He captured the world 5,000- and 10,000-metre records and Olympic titles at these distances. This blond muscular Russian has conquered the pain of running. Few spectators realize the agony a runner can suffer during a distance race, but those who tried to keep up with Kuts's murderous bursts knew the torture all too well. Kuts had an iron character. He is the Communist counterpart of democracy's Herb Elliott.

RON DELANY

Followed Bannister as the master of the 'killer' finish. This won him the Olympic 1,500-metre title. But it was proved that if his strength was sapped early he found it difficult to retaliate. In the race in which I set the world mile record Delany never managed to get within striking distance. He failed in the same way against Herb Elliott. But in most races the sprinting miler succeeds. Delany proved this with his amazing record in indoor events. Here his chopping style and swift acceleration were more effective.

JOHN LANDY

The forerunner of Elliott. He went out from the gun in a mile and still won. These were tactics Elliott never tried in his remarkable season of 1958. Both these brilliant Australians were coached by Percy Cerutty. Landy looked unbeatable until he fell to Bannister in the 1954 Empire Games at Vancouver. As a man, Landy was phlegmatic but made a great impression with his personal integrity.

MERV LINCOLN

Gave up the chance of a promising lawn-tennis career—as a junior he was grouped with Mal Anderson and Ashley Cooper—only to be fated to end up second best in most of his races against Elliott. If he had a weakness it was his inability to apply all his concentration to running. He took up athletics at University only to make up the team, and he always seemed to lack the incentive needed to make a world-beater.

EMIL ZATOPEK

The greatest of them all. He was at the end of his illustrious career when I met him for the only time in Manchester 1955. Every middle and distance runner in the world has accepted his teachings. He was the maestro. To Zatopek, running was always a challenge in itself and the material rewards meant nothing. He even gave away his four Olympic gold medals, saying, 'I do not want to be reminded of my past when I retire.' When he ran his body appeared racked with pain, but this was partly due to his agonized grimace, which meant little. In fact, when the pressure was on the grimace used to vanish as he braced himself to assert his mastery.

22

Tribute to Herb Elliott

> As the field, trailing behind Elliott like the streaming tail
> of a kite, wheeled round the last bend, the Australian seemed
> to find from nowhere an extra reserve of fabulous speed so
> that despite the clearly tremendous pace at which the whole
> race has been run, he finished faster than ever.—*Peter Wilson,
> Daily Mirror*

I FIRST met Herb Elliott at the White City during the A.A.A.
Championships in 1958. He was sitting in the stands with Mike
Agostini, whom I knew well following my visit to Vancouver
earlier that year. Mike, as usual, was sitting with a glamorous
companion—this time a beautiful American blonde.

'Derek, I don't think you have met Herb yet?'

'No, thank the Lord,' I replied. Elliott gave me a grin. 'You've
been running well lately, lad—you must be quite useful,' I told
Elliott.

'You must be going well yourself to have beaten Lincoln in
Vancouver,' Elliott replied.

At the time of this meeting I was still the world's fastest miler—
but my reign was nearly over. And this grinning Aussie was to be
my successor.

During the Empire Games at Cardiff, Herb and I struck up a
close friendship. He visited my home at Huddersfield but it was not
until we were together at the European Championships that I was
able to pinpoint the keystone of his brilliance. It was simply concentration. His running is the god to which everything is sacrificed
when training or competing.

In Stockholm, I lived with a small party of Australians, including
Elliott, in the Swedish team's athletic camp where the facilities were
excellent. There was a swimming-pool, sauna bath, running-track,

and pine forests nearby with paths marked out for cross-country runs. Every day we went training in the morning. Normally there was Dave Power, the 1958 Empire Games marathon champion and six-mile winner, Albie Thomas, a world record holder over two and three miles, Elliott and myself. After a couple of laps on the track to warm up the real stint began, with each of us taking the lead in turn. The pace was always faster when Elliott was in front. And he never stopped for anyone. Training received the same concentrated effort as races. On one occasion Thomas fell and I stopped to help him up. Not Herb. He was away and we didn't see him again that morning.

I don't know whether Elliott liked training because he hardly ever talked athletics. In fact he seldom watched the European Championships, whereas I never missed an important race. Academically, the sport and its personalities did not interest him. If he had not seen Vladimir Kuts win two Olympic titles at Melbourne it is doubtful whether he would ever have been drawn into athletics. He admired the way Kuts went out in front and ran his own race, determined to destroy his rivals. Perhaps the virile ruthlessness of this appealed to Herb. Anyway, these were the tactics he adopted to thrust himself to the pinnacle of athletics fame.

Before a race Elliott never indulges in friendly nods to friends or conventional remarks. The task ahead banishes everything else from his mind. He even refuses to shake hands with his rivals.

'What's the point of being friendly with guys you want to beat?' is his philosophy. 'I shake hands afterwards.'

Behind Elliott is the impish, dynamic personality of Percy Cerutty, who is as much a psychologist as a coach. A modern Spartan, Cerutty still subjects himself to rigorous exercise at the age of sixty-three. That is why he is prepared to drive Elliott to an extremity which would frighten many coaches.

During the morning of the day Elliott broke the world 1,500-metre record (3 min. 36 sec.) Cerutty worked so fanatically on the track that Dana Zatopekova murmured anxiously, 'The old man will collapse.' Afterwards Cerutty wrote Elliott a letter detailing his training schedule, and saying he had run himself to the brink of unconsciousness. 'Tonight,' he added, 'you might run faster than Cerutty—that is the gift of youth—but never harder?'

Cerutty was as excited as a boy when he handed Elliott this

letter over lunch, and whispered to me to watch the expression. Elliott's only reaction was a wry smile but the message had registered. The taunts had served their purpose.

That is how this remarkable partnership has been built up. Europe's classical methods of training and racing, which had ensured domination of the middle distances, have been shunned by these two Australians in pursuit of world conquest. Elliott was easily converted to the doctrine that running must be 'instinctive'. The stop-watch, so long the mentor of runners, was never used. Instead Elliott was instructed to run freely, dominated solely by the animal urge to seek the limits of endurance. In fact it might be said that the Cerutty plan was to dispense with all plans—rather like an Oriental religion.

In races it is the same. Elliott just strives for that sensation of 'liberation' or 'oblivion'. Midway through a race he has whipped himself into a trance and can then remorselessly pull away from the field in what has been described as 'an inhuman display of speed and energy'. Despite his scorn for the stop-watch, Elliott considers anything above four minutes for the mile mediocre.

He is not impressed by his own feats on the track. It is just part of an absorbing research.

Away from the track he is simply a nice guy. He loves children and they love him. When he stayed with me, Christine, then fourteen months, took to him immediately. Occasionally he breaks away from the austere Cerutty schedule. Then he drinks, smokes and attends parties to enable him to return refreshed to battle against the barriers of physical endurance.

Elliott showed the world his dedication to his ideal by turning down a fabulous offer of £90,000 to turn professional. He also declined many invitations to attend an American University on an athletic scholarship, preferring to gain a place at Cambridge University which entailed taking a four-year Latin course in under twelve months.

Together Cerutty and Elliott have brought athletics to the threshold of a new era. They have proved conclusively that not only the body but also the mind must be conquered. Europeans will never recapture the middle-distance records unless they are prepared to follow the same course.

I salute my successor, Herbert John Elliott.

Appendix

TRAINING

During the early days of my athletics career it was generally considered wrong to have a hard cross-country season before competitive track races. In fact, prior to the 1948 Olympic Games in London, British distance runners were officially told not to race over the country as it was thought this would slow them down on the track. Such advice has now been discredited by Stan Eldon, Alain Mimoun (the French 1956 Olympic marathon champion), Gordon Pirie, Frank Sando and John Merriman, to mention just a few. Marathon runners have discovered that their track times over the shorter distances improve after intense training of up to a hundred miles a week. It is significant that my worst season, in 1958, followed a number of poor performances in cross-country races.

This changing attitude with regard to cross-country running shows how theories vary on how to prepare for athletics. There can be no ideal method for everyone, and it is up to each athlete, with the help of his coach, to work out what is best for himself. In this Appendix I have set out the sort of training I have used to prepare myself for track and cross-country racing during the last few seasons.

It must be remembered that this training is designed for world-class performances between one and three miles, and should not be used by a youngster. It is simple to modify it by trial and error. Some runners have to train harder than others, but it is foolish to put all one's best running into preparing for a race. Then you might not be able to produce your best on the big occasion.

There are four variables in training, and if the young athlete bears these in mind, then my own schedules can be converted to his own use. They are:

153

1. *Speed of repetition runs*

   You will see that my training is of the interval type, based on set runs from 220 yards to a mile. Each of these is timed, and should be adjusted according to the stage a competitor has reached in his training.

2. *Speed of recovery*

   Between each run there must be a rest period. This is a vital part of training, and I have discovered that by reducing this to the minimum results on the track have improved. Obviously, the younger athlete needs a longer time to recover.

3. *Number of repetitions*

   The runner soon discovers how long he can train, and what punishment he can absorb. I can use my body as a register.

4. *Distance of the repetitions*

   It is not wise for a young runner to try long distances early in his training. He must build up first, and then increase the distance as his performance and stamina improve. In three miles running it is vital in interval training to cover distances above 440 yards occasionally, i.e. interval 660s and 880s. Others sometimes do three-quarter miles.

Dangers of over-training. I have discovered that this is a subject which engrosses people who know nothing about athletics. A competitor under the age of twenty-one must always be careful because his body is still developing, but after this age it is amazing what punishment can be absorbed without ill-effect. Normally the body itself knows when the 'limit' has been reached, and then training should not be continued. Before starting serious work on schedules a youngster should get advice from a coach—even if it is not possible to receive constant supervision.

I have always had mixed feelings about the value of a personal coach. It is never easy to find the right man, and I have always been sceptical of conventional codes in training. Normally I react to my mood. Often when in London I have visited training-tracks with no prearranged plan in mind. This has encouraged me to experiment with different schedules which, I believe, have helped me in my training. I start with one group of runners, and then join another. This provides variety and adds the spice of competition to avoid boredom.

Summer races are won during winter. That is when the bulk of training must be performed. So often the difficulty is finding the right facilities during these months. In London there are many floodlit tracks, but most provincial athletes are forced to train on the roads or over the country. If this be the case, it is better to use a stretch of land with an unobstructed view as it is then possible to produce an all-out effort over the complete course without stopping at fences or streams. You must always work hard in training to get the best value—quality rather than quantity is the aim. The Hungarian athletes, Iharos, Tabori and Roszavolgi often trained three times a day before the 1956 Olympic Games, but I have never trained more than once a day.

There is no ideal height or weight for an athlete. They come in all sizes, although, within fairly wide limits, there seems to be some uniformity in the top class. When I was a junior I always thought that someone bigger than myself must inevitably win. As a senior, size has never concerned me.

Most leading milers weigh between nine and a half to eleven stone, and have long tapering legs. The heaviest middle-distance runner I remember was Don McMillan, an Australian who reached the Olympic 1,500-metre final at Helsinki. He must have weighed around fourteen stone. Marathon runners are normally small. You don't want to carry a lot of weight on a twenty-six-mile run. Below the mile, the variety in physiques increases. For example, there were striking differences between Tom Courtney and Derek Johnson, who finished first and second in the 800 metres at Melbourne in the last Olympic Games. Courtney is muscular and weighs more than twelve stone, while Johnson is rather frail-looking, and scales less than ten stone. Then there was Arthur Wint, the Jamaican who won the Olympic 400-metre title in 1948; he stood six feet five inches, with a stride of nine feet. Sprinting is basically speed, and this is a gift. Britain's two representatives in the Olympic 100 metres in 1948 were Alastair McCorquindale and McDonald Bailey. McCorquindale was a powerful man who ran mainly on brute strength, while McDonald Bailey was the perfect stylist who had added the art of relaxation to his gift of speed.

Diet. When you are training regularly there is no need to diet to reduce weight. Eat normally but remember that fresh foods are best. It is important not to become too faddy because on overseas trips it might be difficult to get your favourite foods. Views differ about the advisability of eating before races. Many runners still adhere to the traditional poached eggs on toast a few hours before a race. My preference is always for a steak about four hours beforehand. Experience is the best guide for runners on the matter of diet. If possible, try to eat something on the day of the race.

The type of schedules I have worked on during my athletics career are divided into months of the year, as I believe that this is the best approach.

The value of all training depends on first preparing the body. That is why warming-up is so essential. At the start of every session I run for two miles, and follow this with three or four fast bursts over 100 yards to get the blood warm. Exercises are also vital to ensure the muscles are supple for the hard work which is to follow. I suggest the following:

Standing with legs apart, bend while keeping the legs straight, to touch the ground in front and behind the body.

Still in the same position, hold the left ankle with both hands and force the head between the arms six times. Repeat this holding the right ankle. Keep the feet in the same position and swing the left arm sideways. Follow with your head, keeping the right hand on the hip. Do this six times and repeat with the right arm.

Stand with legs apart, and roll trunk in a circular movement several times. Relax the legs by flicking the toes and high kicking in chorus-girl style.

These exercises can be used for all training sessions. It is important that the body is warm, and the heart-beat above normal before starting hard training. All the running muscles must be stretched a few times and relaxed as this prevents the majority of injuries. Many athletes believe they can reduce the length of the training session by cutting down the warm-up. This is false economy. The human body must be prepared for action just like a motor engine, if it is to produce its maximum performance.

After training it is also essential to 'warm-down' for at least a mile, as this helps the body, heart and lungs to recover in a normal fashion.

Never start or stop running with a jerk. This can harm muscles and heart. Another tip: my father used to say that races were won in bed.

Follow exercises with a 200-yard jog, and then training is ready to commence. Here are my schedules:

NOVEMBER AND DECEMBER

Run over open country if possible—otherwise on track or road

First day

Run 880 yards at a time between 2 min. 20 sec. and 2 min. 25 sec. Jog for about 330 yards, taking about 2 min. 30 sec. Repeat at least fifteen times and then warm-down. The total distance of the session —thirteen miles. This includes two miles warming-up and one mile warming-down, which applies to every day of training.

Second day

Run one mile at 4 min. 50 sec. eight times, with a 440-yard jog in between, taking three to three and a half minutes. Distance: twelve and three-quarter miles.

Third day

Fartlek Session (named after the Swedish coach). Run at a fast pace for any distance from 440 yards to a mile, followed by a short jog. The idea of this exercise is to travel as fast as the mind and body allow. Cover at least ten miles.

Fourth day

Same as the first day.

Fifth day

Ten runs over three-quarters of a mile in 3 min. 55 sec., broken by three-minute jogs over 440 yards. Distance: twelve and three-quarter miles.

Sixth day

Another Fartlek Session. It may be that on this day you have a competition, but at this time of the year it is not a good idea to take a rest. However, should you be involved in a first-class race, it is essential to have a break from training.

Seventh day

In my case this would be a day off (Sunday), and I usually take a long morning walk which helps mental recuperation. I would play a game of golf or tennis, or if the weather is bad a game of squash. Such games should be taken as recreation and not as highly competitive affairs.

Repeat this weekly programme until January.

JANUARY AND FEBRUARY

First day

Run 880 yards at a speed of 2 min. 15 sec. to 2 min. 20 sec. If you have no track, then run the equivalent distance either on the road or across flat country. Follow this by a slow jog of a distance between 200 and 300 yards, taking a time of two to two and a half minutes. Repeat this until fifteen half-miles have been completed. Don't forget the warming-up and warming-down periods. Distance: twelve and a half miles.

Second day

Run three-quarter-mile stretches at a pace of 3 min. 25 sec. to 3 min. 30 sec. Jog for 300 to 400 yards in between each three-quarter-mile. Do at least ten with interval jogging of between two and a half to three minutes. Distance: twelve and a quarter miles.

Third day
Fartlek Session.

Fourth day

As this would sometimes be the last day of training before a big cross-country race, such as county or area championships, then the training should not be tough. Run a series of 660 yards at a speed of 1 min. 40 sec. to 1 min. 45 sec. Jog for a distance of 200 to 300 yards, taking two to two and a half minutes. Repeat fourteen times. Distance covered, ten miles.

Fifth day

Rest.

Sixth day

Race.

Seventh day

Easy run over about six to seven miles, to take the stiffness out of the body from the previous day's competition.

If at this time of the year the sixth day is not a race day, then the schedule should be as follows:

Fifth day

Run one mile in a time of 4 min. 40 sec., with a jog of about 440 yards in between, taking three minutes. Do nine of these. Total distance of fourteen miles.

Sixth day

Personally I would use this for a run with the local harriers, and cover about twelve miles or so over rough country.

Seventh day

Day off, although occasionally I have felt like training hard on this day and would then go into the woods near my home in Huddersfield to find a steep hill. After my usual warm-up, I would run up and down the wooded slope and in between jog for about two minutes. This helps to increase the power of the legs.

For most athletes weight-training can be a great asset during the *winter*. I have done little myself, but then I've a belief that my environment has helped to make me strong. However, I have found weights useful for strengthening my stomach muscles, as below:

These exercises can be performed by lying on the ground and holding the weight behind the head. Then lift the head, arms and weight over the body, and touch legs below the knees. Repeat this fifteen times. Then use bar weight-lifting with a weight which is manageable. Raise from behind the shoulders to the full stretch of the arms twelve times. It is a good idea to repeat these exercises three times after four training sessions a week.

MARCH—FIRST TWO WEEKS

The first two weeks of this month cover the end of the cross-country season. After this one must get ready for the track, and put in some speed work. The exercises and warm-up should be as before.

First day

880 yards eight times, in 2 min. 16 sec., with a jog of 330 yards or so in three minutes. Follow this with 440 yards six times at an average of 67 seconds. Break this up with a jog of 250 yards over two minutes. Total distance: ten and three-quarter miles. Don't forget the warm-up, preliminary exercises and warm-down.

Second day

660 yards fourteen times in 1 min. 42 sec., with a 300-yard jog of two and a half minutes in between. Total distance of ten and a half miles.

Third day

440 yards twenty times in a time of 68 seconds, broken by jogs of 440 yards in approximately two minutes. This reduction in the time for the jog is aimed at improving performances during racing. Total distance: twelve and three-quarter miles.

Some runners take a five-minute jog, which is no good for top-class performances as it is conducive to laziness. Also the pulse rate drops too much, and reverts to normal, therefore increasing the strain on the heart. A fast jog keeps the system ticking over better, and avoids sudden changes in the pulse rate. This is strictly *à la Ibbotson*, and not something I have discovered from coaches or books, although I believe it to be common sense.

Fourth day

This would normally be around the time of a cross-country championship, and if competing you are advised to take it fairly easily with eight to ten miles Fartlek in 1 hr. 10 min. If not running at the week-end, then repeat the first day's routine.

Fifth day

Rest if competing; Fartlek if not.

Sixth day

Race or training run with club over ten miles.

Seventh day

If stiff, then I would advise a gentle run. Those in good condition might try running up hills or a long walk, followed by a game of golf or tennis.

MARCH—THIRD AND FOURTH WEEKS

Now is the time to turn over to serious track training. If a floodlit stadium is not available then you are advised to work on the roads.

L

Every big town in Britain should boast a floodlit track. At the London County Council ground at Tooting Bec Common at least a hundred athletes turn out during the early spring to prepare for the summer season. In such an atmosphere it is possible to work much harder.

First day

15 × 440 yards in 68 seconds, with a jog in between of 220 yards taking two minutes or so. Try to keep to these times. Do not run 70 seconds, and then say to yourself, 'The soft track lost me one second and a strong wind another second.' It will only lull you into a false sense of fitness.

Second day

12 × 660 yards in 1 min. 42 sec., with jogs of 350 yards in between of three minutes.

Third day

As on first day.

Fourth day

12 × 440 yards in 68 seconds. Jog for 220 yards in between in two minutes. 8 × 220 yards in 33 sec., with a 220-yard jog in two minutes.

Fifth day

As second day.

Sixth day

Road race or repeat first day.

Seventh day

Long walk, golf or tennis. If you are behind in training, then I suggest 10 × 440 yards in 68 seconds, with 220-yard jogs of two minutes. Also 4 × 220 yards in 33 seconds, with a 220-yard jog of two minutes.

Now you have got used to the track training again, try and increase or decrease three of the variables in training:

1. Increase the number of repetitions.
2. Decrease the recovery period.
3. Decrease the actual time of the repetition runs.

I have discovered that most leading athletes find they have an 'overdrive' when training over repetition quarter-miles. This happens after the first two or three runs. After about fifty yards it is possible to relax the legs, stretch them and, still putting in the same power, go faster—just like changing gear or slipping into an 'overdrive'.

First day

20 × 440 yards in 60 seconds. Jog 220 yards in one and three-quarter minutes.

Second day

16 × 660 yards in 1 min. 40 secs. Jog 330 yards in two and a half minutes.

Third day

As first day.

Fourth day

16 × 440 yards in 65 seconds. Jog 220 yards in one and three-quarter minutes. 8 × 220 yards in 32·5 seconds, with a 300-yard jog in one and three-quarter minutes.

Fifth day

10 × 880 yards in 2 min. 12 sec. Jog of 440 yards in 1 min. 35 sec.

Sixth day

As first day.

Seventh day

Rest day. Walking, golf, tennis, swimming or a run in the woods of six miles at an enjoyable speed.

Carry on this training for another week and then change as follows:

First day

20 × 440 yards in 64 seconds. Jog 220 yards in 1 min. 15 sec.

Second day

16 × 660 yards in 1 min. 36 sec. Jog of 330 yards in 1 min. 45 sec.

Third day

As first day.

Fourth day

16 × 440 yards in 63 seconds. Jog of 220 yards in 70 seconds. 10 × 220 yards in 31·5 seconds. Then a jog of 220 yards of 70 seconds.

Fifth day

12 × 880 yards in 2 min. 10 sec. Jog of 440 yards in 1 min. 30 sec.

Sixth day

As first day.

Seventh day

As previously in April.

First day

20 × 440 yards in 62 seconds. Jog in between of 220 yards in one and a quarter minutes. Warm-up and down as before.

Second day

16 × 660 yards in 1 min. 34 sec., with jog of 330 yards in 1 min. 30 sec.

Third day

As first day.

Fourth day

12 × 880 yards in 2 min. 8 sec. Jog 440 yards in between of 1 min. 25 sec.

Fifth day

30 × 220 yards in 29 seconds, with 220-yard jog of 60 seconds.

Sixth day

As first day.

Seventh day

As previously.

MAY—FIRST WEEK

First day

20 × 440 yards in 60 seconds. Jog of 220 yards in 60 seconds.

Second day

16 × 660 yards in 1 min. 32 sec. Jog of 330 yards in 1 min. 20 sec.

Third day

24 × 440 yards in 60 seconds. Jog of 220 yards in 60 seconds.

Fourth day

12 × 880 yards in 2 min. 5 sec. Jog 440 yards in 1 min. 25 sec.

Fifth day

Sharpen speed with 12 × 440 yards in 58 seconds. Jog 110 yards in 50 seconds.

Sixth day

As third day.

Seventh day

As previously.

Now you should be racing every Saturday and so the schedules should be made out accordingly.

Here is my idea of preparing for a race, commencing at 3.30 p.m.:

Breakfast at 9. am.
Lunch at noon. Not too heavy. Not too much liquid.
At the track. You should be at the track at least three-quarters of an hour before the competition. Always take two pairs of spikes—one for a hard track and one for a soft.
At 2.55 p.m. change and start warming-up by jogging slowly for a quarter of a mile, then faster for another six minutes or so. Then perform one of the exercises I have recommended in the earlier part

of the Appendix. Follow this by intermittent sprints of fifty or sixty yards.

At 3.17 p.m. return to the dressing-room to get spikes, and to attend to personal needs. Rub down and sweat off. Go on the track and put on spikes five minutes before the race. Jog about to make sure spikes are comfortable.

MAY—SECOND WEEK

First day

20 × 440 yards in 60 seconds. Jog in between of 110 yards in 50 seconds.

Second day

16 × 660 yards in 1 min. 30 sec. Jog of 220 yards in 1 min. 15 sec.

Third day

24 × 440 yards in 60 seconds. Jog of 110 yards in 50 seconds.

Fourth day

12 × 880 yards in 2 min. 3 sec. Jog 330 yards in 1 min. 15 sec.

Fifth day

Rest before major competition. Before a minor race do 12 × 440 yards in 58 seconds. Jog of 110 yards in 50 seconds.

Sixth day

Race.

Seventh day

As previously. If you have not competed, then 16 × 440 yards in 60 seconds, with a jog of 110 yards.

First day

24 × 440 yards in 60 seconds. Jog of 110 yards in 45 seconds.

Second day

18 × 660 yards in 1 min. 30 sec. Jog of 440 yards in 1 min. 30 sec.

Third day

As first day

Fourth day

16 × 440 yards in 58 seconds. Jog of 110 yards in 45 seconds.

Fifth day

Rest if before a major competition. If competing in a minor race, then 12 × 440 yards in 58 seconds. Jog of 110 yards in 45 seconds.

Sixth day

Race.

Seventh day

Rest, or 16 × 440 yards in 60 seconds, and jogs of 110 yards in 65 seconds.

For the rest of the season these schedules can be used and varied accordingly. For example, before the A.A.A. Championships use the seventh-day training schedule for the fourth day, and rest on the fifth and sixth days.

Never worry if you have to miss a training session, but don't do it too often.

Finally, some athletes suffer from slight stomach pains when training. Always remember that to fight these off is a victory of mind over body which is of tremendous importance. If you retire in training then remember that in a race when you are really suffering you will do just the same.

Courage wins races.

Index